NO MORE
BEDWETTING

NO MORE BEDWETTING

How to Help Your Child Stay Dry

Samuel J. Arnold, M.D., F.A.C.S.

John Wiley & Sons, Inc.

New York • Chichester • Weinheim • Brisbane • Singapore • Toronto

Library of Congress Cataloging-in-Publication Data

Arnold, Samuel J.
    No more bedwetting : how to help your child stay dry / Samuel J. Arnold.
        p.   cm.
    Includes bibliographical references and index.
    ISBN 0-471-14690-0 (pbk. : alk. paper)
    1. Enuresis—Popular works. 2. Enuresis—Prevention. I. Title.
RJ476.E6A76 1997
618.92'849—dc21   97-21709
                                                CIP

Printed in the United States of America

10 9 8 7 6 5 4 3 2 1

To my wife Catherine, my daughters Bonnie and Lisa, and my son Michael—the wellsprings of great happiness.

ACKNOWLEDGMENTS

I would like to thank Ruth McWhinney, Jean Allison, Hazel Edwards, and Sylvia Wexler—my office staff of many years; Dr. Arthur Ginsburg—my partner of twenty-five years; Merrill Harvey and Brian Pendley for art; Dr. Stuart Levy and Miss Sue Sanchelli for bringing me up-to-date on parental participation in anesthetizing children; M. Robert Aaron and Professor Jim Kaiser for checking my concepts of fluid flow; and Dr. Michael Arnold and Professor Mary Louise Hayden for tempering the "medicalese" of my prose.

And very special thanks to Jo Anne Searly, Mary Kay Joyce, and James Dvoretzky and Thelma Fitch of Morristown Memorial Health Sciences Library; to Dr. David Copp and Mr. Edward Pikus for help over and beyond the call of friendship; and to Lila Hunnewell for bringing the book home.

CONTENTS

INTRODUCTION

A child's bedwetting can be a baffling and frustrating fact of life for the whole family. It tries the patience of the most well-meaning parents, and it torments the bedwetting child. Many parents mistakenly believe that bedwetting is a deliberate failure to get out of bed by a "lazy," "careless," "disobedient," or "immature" child. As a result, long-term bedwetting creates feelings of anger, shame, and confusion—feelings that pull families apart and cause children to become unfortunate victims of emotional and even physical abuse, with serious damage to their self-esteem, family relationships, and social life.

I would like to share with you the story of how I became aware that long-term bedwetting from birth is caused not by psychological or maturational problems but by *physical* factors that are beyond the child's control—most of which factors are treatable—and why I have felt it necessary to write this book.

About 35 years ago, I believed (along with most doctors of that period) that if no urinary infection was present, bedwetting, along with daytime urinary problems such as frequent running to the bathroom, difficulty making it to the bathroom "in time," and spotting underpants with urine, were mainly psychological in origin. Because I was a urological surgeon rather than a psychiatrist, I did not encourage pediatricians and general practitioners to refer bedwetting children to me for treatment: I felt that I could help only a few.

To spare the majority of bedwetting children and their parents the stress (and expense) of "needless" urological examinations, I designed a questionnaire that could be filled out by the children's doctor and the parents, which I thought would allow me, without examining the children, to identify the few wetters who might require urological treatment. I felt that the rest of the bedwetting children could continue to be treated by their pediatricians (who might refer them to psychologists or psychiatrists).

The questionnaire I designed probed for both psychological problems (such as sibling rivalry, anxieties, or too much parental discipline) and physical problems (such as pus in the urine, fever, pain on urination, or other difficulties with urination). I assumed that if the child had no fever or pus in the urine, and if any possibility of an emotional problem existed, then the basis for the wetting was psychological.

I distributed the blank questionnaires to my referring pediatricians and general doctors and asked them to send me only the completed forms, not the children.

The method failed. Some children who I did not examine because their questionnaires suggested psychological problems developed urinary infections. Others remained wetters despite the best efforts of their pediatricians and the psychologists to whom they were referred. At last I began examining the children themselves. To my surprise, I found physical problems in the majority of them. Sometimes I found easily detectable physical problems, but most often I found subtle ones—small abnormalities such as narrowings or constrictions in the urethra (the tube leading from the bladder to the outside). These small abnormalities were easily corrected through minor surgical procedures, which, I soon discovered, relieved the daytime urinary symptoms in a high percentage of cases almost immediately (so that the child no longer had to rush to the bathroom to avoid daytime "accidents") and relieved the night-wetting in a highly significant percentage of cases within a few months.

In treating my first bedwetting child, I began to question the thinking of the time about the causes of bedwetting. A family physician had sent me a questionnaire he obtained from the mother of a nine-year-old bedwetter. From the completed questionnaire, I learned that the boy, who had been difficult to toilet-train, wet his bed every night. During the day, he spotted his underpants with urine and dashed often to the bathroom, clutching his penis, sometimes not getting to the toilet in time. The boy did poorly at school and had frequent temper tantrums.

The mother was divorced and sharing their home with a man whom she planned to marry. As I read the questionnaire, it occurred to me that the mother's relationship with this man may have caused the boy emotional distress, and thus the bedwetting. Without seeing the boy, I recommended to the referring physician that the boy get psychological counseling.

While the mother considered this recommendation, the boy happened to take a routine urine test for school athletics, which revealed pus in the urine. The mother took the child back to the child's doctor, who referred him to me. Because of the pus in the urine, I agreed to see him.

On examining the boy, I found that his penis had an extremely narrow opening and his urethra was somewhat inflamed. After I corrected this simple physical problem by enlarging the opening, the boy's urine cleared of pus, and his urethra returned to normal. In addition, he no longer needed to rush to the bathroom, no longer needed to urinate frequently, and no longer wet the bed except when he was overly tired or catching a cold. Even his temper tantrums disappeared. I saw that not the pus in the urine, but the narrowing of the penile opening that led to the inflamed urethra was the cause of both the wetting and the urinary infection.

This experience prompted me to read every piece of medical literature I could find on the subject of abnormal narrowings or constrictions of the penile opening. I found that several eminent urologists of the past (particularly Meredith Campbell—the "father of pediatric urology") had described how such minor abnormalities could produce bedwetting and daytime symptoms (even if the urine contained *no* pus).

I decided to undertake my own study of 160 hospital charts of boys who had been diagnosed as having such narrowings. Like the published material I had read, my study of the hospital records showed clearly that these constrictions could make a child urinate much too often, rush to the bathroom, and wet the bed. Such constrictions also led to irritable erections—that is, erections caused not by erotic play or self-stimulation, but by inflammation and irritation of the nerve endings. I published my findings in the *Journal of Urology* to inform the medical community.

Unfortunately, the paper with my findings failed to reach enough members of the urological community. If the patient's urine did not contain pus or blood, most physicians continued to blame bedwetting and daytime urinary symptoms on emotional factors, imperceptible nervous system disease, or "irritable bladders."

During this time, my experience with bedwetting children and my knowledge about bedwetting increased rapidly. Among other things, I learned from a majority of the parents that their bedwetting children slept so heavily that they could scarcely awaken them, even with noise, lights, shaking, and lifting. I learned that the majority of the night-wetters who came to see me also had daytime urinary symptoms. In addition, I noted that in children with such daytime symptoms, not only small penile openings but also a number of other small urethral abnormalities that many doctors dismissed as "variants of normal" or as "not significant," actually *did* also cause or contribute to bedwetting. Finally, I learned from the work of researchers Richards P. Lyon and Donald R. Smith, published in the *Journal of Urology*, that other small abnormalities occurred in girls; these, too, caused bedwetting.

When I questioned parents who had themselves experienced bedwetting along with daytime urinary problems in childhood, I learned that, contrary to general opinion, bedwetters did not necessarily outgrow their disorders. Far more men who had been bedwetters as children suffered later in life with inflammation of the prostate and the urethra than did nonwetters. They also tended to have sexual symptoms, such as painful and/or premature (overly rapid) ejaculations.

Women who were former wetters often complained of involuntary loss of urine when they coughed, sneezed, or strained to do various tasks. Many experienced recurring urinary infections, vaginal irritations, and pain with intercourse. Many former wetters of both sexes still had to awaken from one to three times a night to urinate. During the day, they still had to urinate frequently, often having to rush to the bathroom for fear of wetting themselves. In other words, they had "outgrown" their bedwetting, but the physical abnormalities that had caused their wetting still caused problems.

Local physicians, particularly pediatricians, were delighted that a urologist finally showed an interest in bedwetting, and they sent me many patients. When I had accumulated data on 187 cases of my own, I presented my findings at the Sixtieth Annual Meeting of the American Urological Association, in New Orleans. My presentation was received coolly, although it was reported in the news section of the *Journal of the American Medical Association*. In addition to their general lack of interest in bedwetting, other urologists could not conceive of the significance of the small abnormalities that I found so instrumental in bedwetting.

The data I accumulated had enabled me to formulate three hypotheses:

1. Psychological problems rarely (if ever) cause persistent bedwetting from birth.
2. A bedwetter who also has persistent daytime urinary symptoms has a physical condition, mostly in the lower urinary organs.
3. A heavy-sleep factor prevents the bedwetter from awakening to urinate. (The child who has daytime urinary symptoms but not an un-

usually heavy sleep pattern awakens—sometimes several times—to go to the bathroom at night instead of wetting the bed.)

My studies also allowed me to conclude that the more careful the doctor's physical and urological examination of the bedwetting patient, the more likely a physical cause for the bedwetting would be found. At the same time, I saw that the minority of bedwetters who did *not* have daytime urinary symptoms (urgency, frequency, loss of urine) could not be treated urologically. They did not have physical abnormalities in the urinary tract. (The causes of long-term wetting in children who do not have daytime symptoms are also physical rather than psychological: unusually deep sleep; deficiency of the hormone vasopressin; intolerances to foods or other substances; and other physical causes.)

My experience with bedwetting children continued to grow and to reinforce my findings. Soon, Dr. Arthur Ginsburg joined me in practice and, working with his own patients, confirmed what I had reported. When our combined experience with bedwetters reached approximately five hundred cases, we presented our new study at the annual meeting of the American Medical Association. Still, most urologists remained skeptical of the role of small urethral abnormalities in bedwetting and daytime urinary symptoms.

But Dr. Ginsburg and I continued our studies and often presented our findings so that other doctors, too, could use our methods to help many more bedwetting children. We published a first-time-ever photostudy that matched up X rays of bladders and urethras with photographs taken through a cystourethroscope (pronounced sis-toh-yoo-re-throh-scohp), the instrument that urologists use to look inside the bladder and urethra. With these pictures we were able to show the following things: the areas we considered problem areas, such as small urethral folds, flaps, and narrowings (constrictions); the simple operations used to correct these abnormalities; and the changes the operations produced as seen on follow-up X rays. We were able to explain the connections (in most cases) between the surgical changes and the relief or lessening of the bedwetters' symptoms. After the publication of this study, several urologists wrote to tell us that they had used our techniques and had similar experiences with patients.

Unfortunately, many physicians and the general public still cling to the theory that bedwetting from birth is psychological, and in doing so they perpetuate the frustration and misery of millions of bedwetters and their families.

Here is a case in point. An 11-year-old boy, desperate about his bedwetting, wrote to a nationally syndicated, well-respected advice columnist, asking for her help. He described himself as the unhappiest person in the world because he had been unable to stop bedwetting no matter how hard he tried. He had even tried starving himself and going without water for days at a time. His mother had taken him to a doctor, who reassured her that her son had no disease and would outgrow the problem. When the mother heard that the son had no physical disease, she tried to disgrace him out of his bedwetting by telling everyone that her "11-year-old baby boy" still wet the bed. The boy concluded his letter with a promise to follow the columnist's advice, no matter what it might be.

The columnist answered that many adolescents wet the bed because they are insecure and unhappy and suggested that the boy's parents take him to a doctor who could "work out emotional problems." How unfortunate that this total misconception was passed on to many millions of readers.

Over the years, I have taken other opportunities to share my experiences and findings. Doctors Willet Whitmore, John Lattimer, David Utz, and Pablo Morales, who were nationally known chiefs of urology at Sloan-Kettering, Columbia Presbyterian, Mayo Clinic, and New York University Medical School, gave me opportunities to express my views. Dr. Frank Field, when he was with NBC-TV, gave me a chance to air my opinions nationally and locally.

The rewards for my efforts to understand and treat bedwetting and other urinary problems in children have come from the children themselves and from their families. Children, free of the embarrassment of bedwetting, have blossomed. Their reactions have been touching and heartwarming. A first-grader sent me a carefully printed note on lined paper decorated with her drawings of flowers:

Dear Dr. Arnold,

Thank you for helping me with my problem. I slept over at my friend's house, for the first time. . . .

Letters such as the one from a former patient describing her feelings about having been cured of bedwetting are great sources of professional satisfaction to me:

Dear Dr. Arnold,

This letter is terribly overdue . . . about eight years overdue
. . . . I have just taken it for granted all these years that I am able
to do all the things I want to do because you helped me. It was
an amazing thing how one day I was being beaten for wetting
my pants, and then the next I was cured—totally. And I have
had no problems at all since then. I no longer have to . . . be
embarrassed [by hearing] in front of my friends what I did and
that I did it because I wanted attention. . . .

I will never forget the embarrassment, humiliation, and utter
despair that I went through. I still remember everything today.
. . . I can talk openly about it, and I am really surprised at how
many people went through the same thing I did. I feel lucky that
my problem was taken care of when I was young, although I
wish it had been taken care of even earlier.

I am very happy now. I was really miserable before my parents brought me to you, after all the other doctors told me I was
"just lazy." I am not lazy now, so I know I wasn't lazy then. I
have worked since I have been old enough to work, and I just
graduated from college with a Bachelor's in Fine Arts.

I am 22 years old now, still single, and having a "blast." I go
out to parties and to other people's homes, and I travel. I have
been to Europe twice. In June, I will go to Greece for two months.
The most wonderful thing is that I can go anywhere without
worrying about wetting. . . .

I do want to thank you again. Thanks.

Sincerely,

Althea

Parents, relieved of guilt (and laundry burdens), have also been
thrilled to have their children cured. An example is a letter from a mother
in Indiana who had read one of my articles in a medical journal and
taken her son to a urologist who (perhaps guided by the article) enlarged
a narrow area within the boy's urethra and cured him. With her note, she
sent me a photograph of her very cheerful-looking son.

Correspondence came from very distant places. A lady in Australia,
for example, wrote to ask for copies of my articles, and then later wrote
to thank me. It appeared that over time she had taken her daughter to five

different doctors to treat the girl's bedwetting and daytime urinary symptoms. Of the five doctors who examined the girl, not one suggested that she should see a urologist. They blamed the girl's symptoms on "laziness," "stubbornness," and "jealousy" over her newborn baby sister. They reassured the mother that the daughter would "outgrow" her symptoms. After receiving the articles, the mother consulted a urologist who quickly cured the child by removing a minor physical obstruction.

I have great faith in the ability of people supplied with facts to arrive at logical conclusions. Unfortunately, too many books about bedwetting written for parents, and too many urological textbooks as well, ignore the weighty evidence for physical factors that cause or contribute to night-wetting and daytime symptoms. Having conducted extensive research into the causes and treatments of bedwetting and having had high levels of success in treating approximately two thousand children who wet the bed, I have written this book to inform parents and other concerned caregivers who have struggled so long to understand what causes bedwetting and what can be done about it.

1

BEDWETTING AND YOUR CHILD

Your child wets his bed, and you have "tried everything" to help him stop. Very likely, you have made many efforts at "behavior modification," such as giving special rewards for a dry bed or punishments for a wet bed—or giving your child the "responsibility" of changing, washing, and hanging the sheets when you discovered a wet bed. Perhaps you asked your bedwetter to "envision" a dry bed before going to sleep, or to employ other imaging methods or positive thoughts. All to no avail!

This book will show you that efforts aimed at behavior modification—punishing, shaming, cajoling, bribing, rewarding, or otherwise training your long-term bedwetter to keep the bed dry—cannot work! Your child does not choose to wet the bed any more than he chooses to develop appendicitis. He does not wet because of laziness, irresponsibility, or hostility. And he does not wet because of immaturity, delayed toilet training, or habit.

This book will inform you that most bedwetting starts at birth and that the causes of bedwetting from birth are physical. Most bedwetting is caused by *underlying physical conditions.*

Most important, this book will assure you that almost all childhood bedwetting can be cured or controlled. It will inform you of the causes (there are many), provide a systematic method for discovering the one that underlies your own child's bedwetting, and enable you to get effective treatment.

HOW TO USE THIS BOOK

It is important for you to read the entire book, in the order in which the chapters are presented, to obtain a complete picture of the many different causes of bedwetting. Do not skip any chapters. After the first reading, go back and begin again, this time investigating the possible causes of your child's bedwetting in the order in which they are presented.

First, finish this chapter, which provides some of the answers to your general questions about bedwetting, as well as definitions of important terms.

Next, read chapter 2, because it provides simple explanations of the anatomy and physiology that you need to know to understand many of the succeeding chapters.

Then read chapter 3. Heavy sleep often plays a contributing role in bedwetting (no matter what the principal cause); you need to know what this chapter says about the role of heavy sleep and sleep disturbances before you read later chapters.

Next, read chapter 4, which describes certain diseases that you and your child's doctor need to rule out first, even though most bedwetting is not caused by them.

Chapter 5 asks you if your child's present bedwetting appeared after a period of dryness of at least six months (during which time your child was not assisted to the toilet at night). If so, this is the time to follow the suggested strategies for dealing with renewed wetting (different from wetting from birth).

If factors discussed in the previous chapters are found not to be the cause of your child's bedwetting, you should next follow the recommendations in chapter 6 to investigate constipation, hemorrhoids, and anal inflammation, any of which can be responsible for bedwetting (either from birth or after a period of dryness).

If the problems described in chapter 6 are not to blame, take the next appropriate step and follow the suggestions in chapter 7: detecting and addressing any allergies or food intolerances that may be causing your child's bedwetting. Because this is a complicated process, it is undertaken after the preceding factors have been ruled out.

I hope you will have found the cause of your child's wetting through the methods recommended in earlier chapters, but if not, chapter 8 explains how a nighttime shortage of a hormone, vasopressin, can cause bedwetting from birth. If your child does not need to urinate frequently or with urgency in the daytime (which would point to other causes), you can now consider a visit to a doctor who can start treating your child with a wetness alarm or with the synthetic hormone desmopressin. This step is left until late in your investigation to make sure other causes are ruled out before your child begins a long course of medication.

Chapter 9 shows you how, from birth, small obstructions in the urethra can cause both bedwetting and the frequent and urgent need to urinate in the daytime. You should rule out all other possible causes before investigating this one because the examination and treatment may require anesthesia and surgical procedures in a hospital setting.

Finally, you need to know what steps to take in preparing your child for the visit to the family doctor or pediatrician; the possible visit to a urologist or other specialist; and, if necessary, a procedure in the hospital. Read chapter 10 to familiarize yourself with these steps.

Throughout your reading, you will see mentions of studies that support the ideas presented in this book. Almost all were conducted by physicians and professors engaged in advanced research and were reported in medical journals or books. If you are interested in any articles, see, at the end of this book, the Bibliography, arranged alphabetically by authors' last names. You can try to obtain the journal or book in which the article was published from the library of a local hospital or medical school. (Most public libraries do not carry medical research literature.)

In addition to the studies mentioned in the chapters, the Bibliography also includes the names of many articles and books that are not mentioned in the text but that provided me with useful background information about the topics addressed. If you (or your doctors) wish to know more about a particular topic, you can scan the list for titles that are related to it. Perhaps your doctor can obtain the articles for you through the library of the hospital with which he is affiliated.

WHAT IS BEDWETTING?

The inability to control urination during the day or during the night is a condition that has a medical name: *enuresis*. A person who wets involuntarily at any time is said to be *enuretic*. A person who wets at night during sleep suffers from *nocturnal enuresis*, or bedwetting. However, since most involuntary wetting occurs at night, many people refer to bedwetting simply as "enuresis." If your doctor uses that term, it generally means bedwetting.

AT WHAT AGE DOES NORMAL INFANT WETTING BECOME BEDWETTING?

Toddlers stop wetting at different ages, so there is some debate about when your child's wetting is no longer the normal wetting of an infant. However, everyone can agree that if your child is still wetting more than occasionally at age five or six (which is about two or three years after the large majority of children have stopped), you should begin to investigate the cause of the wetting.

DOES BEDWETTING RUN IN FAMILIES?

Yes, the underlying physical causes of bedwetting do tend to run in families! I have treated families where a parent and two children wet the bed. I knew a family in which nine children all wet the bed every night! Bedwetters may have been found in three or four generations.

In addition to my own observations, the research of others shows this inherited relationship. Studies by Harry Bakwin found that in families where both parents were bedwetters as children, 77 percent of the children were also bedwetters; where one parent was a bedwetter, 43 percent of the children were bedwetters. And if one child in an identical set of twins was a bedwetter, the other twin wet in 68 percent of cases, while in nonidentical twins the figure was 36 percent.

Søren Wille's study, published in the Swedish journal *Lakartidningen*, found that 70 percent of bedwetting children (compared with 24 percent of nonbedwetting children) had family members or close relatives who were enuretic. And J. B. J. McKendry and colleagues found a wider gap—80 percent of bedwetting children (compared with 15 percent of nonbedwetters) had a parent, sibling, aunt, uncle, or grandparent who was enuretic. (Enuretic children are often surprised—and relieved—to learn that one or both of their parents also wet in childhood.)

Most recently, research published by Hans Eiberg of Denmark in *Nature Genetics* (1995) indicates that a gene (on chromosome 13) is linked to at least one cause of primary bedwetting. (Interestingly, as Eiberg told Daniel Goleman of *The New York Times*, no pattern of inheritance was found for secondary bedwetting.) The newly discovered gene is not linked to the shortage of the hormone vasopressin.

In light of the inherited nature of primary bedwetting, if either you or your spouse were bedwetters, it is likely that one or more of your children will be bedwetters, too. You should not be reluctant to share this information with your child to help him realize that you are sympathetic to the problem.

HOW MANY BEDWETTERS ARE THERE?

There are many more bedwetters than most people believe. Various studies have tried to determine the number, with varied results. An overview of these studies, undertaken by Dr. Larry G. McLain (in his book *Current Problems in Pediatrics: Childhood Enuresis*), suggests that at ages three to four about 20 to 30 percent of all children wet their beds; at age five, about 15 percent; at age six, about 6 to 7 percent. According to the overview, wetting continues to decrease until, at age ten, perhaps 3.25 percent still wet. Approximately 2 percent of enuretics continue to wet in adult life.

In the United States, estimates of the number of bedwetters range from 5 million to 10 million. According to researcher Linda Shortliffe, about 20 percent of bedwetting children are enuretic during the day as well.

The true numbers, however, are likely to be significantly higher, because so much bedwetting is unreported. Many parents simply do not confide this information about their children, even to the children's doctors. Many adult enuretics are also too embarrassed to reveal this problem to their doctors. Since bedwetting remains a "closet condition," we have no way of knowing the size of the unreported group.

Although researchers do not agree on the numbers, most agree that more boys than girls wet their beds.

ARE THERE DIFFERENT TYPES OF BEDWETTERS?

Doctors place bedwetters in categories. If your child has wet from birth and never stopped, she is called a *primary enuretic*. Most bedwetters are primary enuretics.

If your child begins to wet again after having been dry for about six months or more, she is called a *secondary enuretic*. There are important differences between these two groups.

Primary Wetting

If your child has been wetting since birth, her wetting almost certainly has physical causes, not psychological causes. There are many physical causes of primary wetting, including a variety of diseases, heavy sleep, sleep disturbances, chronic constipation, allergies or food intolerances, shortage of the hormone vasopressin, and small obstructions or constrictions in the urethra. (Much more will be said in later chapters about all of the causes mentioned in chapter 1.)

Secondary Wetting

If your child has begun bedwetting after about six months or more of being dry (secondary wetting), he may simply be experiencing a temporary episode caused by infection, illness, a medication, or excessive fluid intake. He may be suffering from pinworms or the onset of diabetes. Or he may be experiencing a major change in life that he finds very threatening or overwhelming. Secondary wetting is the only type of bedwetting that may have psychological causes.

According to a study of bedwetting children conducted by Canadian researchers J. B. J. McKendry and colleagues and according to Linda Shortliffe, one-quarter to one-third of all bedwetters are secondary wetters.

Daytime Urinary Symptoms

In addition to primary and secondary wetting, doctors place bedwetting into other categories. One of the most important relates to daytime urinary symptoms. Bedwetting that occurs in children who need to urinate frequently and urgently during the daytime is different from bedwetting that occurs in children who have no such need. There are some very important differences between these two types of wetting.

When Daytime Symptoms Are Present

Many children who wet the bed are primary enuretics (bedwetters from birth) *who also have one or more long-term, daytime urinary symptoms.* Go through this list to see if your child has any of these symptoms during the day:

Frequency. Does your child have to urinate more often than other children? This is one of the most typical daytime urinary symptoms.

Urgency. During the daytime, can your child avoid an accident only by dashing to the bathroom the moment he feels the urge to urinate? (Parents often think that children with this symptom are "waiting until the last moment" to go to the toilet, but this is not so. The need to urinate is urgent at the first moment or within the first few moments.) A study conducted by Canadian researchers J. B. J. McKendry and associates and published in the journal *Applied Therapeutics* shows that 60 percent of bedwetting children experience daytime urgency.

Spotting or wetting. During the daytime, is your child sometimes (or often) unable get to the toilet in time, so that his underclothing becomes spotted or wet with urine? McKendry's group found that 39 percent of bedwetting children experience daytime dribbling. In addition, does your child wet himself while coughing, sneezing, laughing, or straining?

Jigging up and down, sitting or bouncing on the heels, rocking to and fro, crossing the legs with great pressure, or clutching the genitals. Does your child do any of these things in an effort to hold back the urine? (Some parents mistake "clutching" for masturbation, which it is not. "Clutching" is simply an attempt to prevent dribbling or urination. Most of the time, children are not even aware that they are doing it.) See figure 1.1 for typical ways children try to control the urge to urinate.

Unusual urination. Does your child strain or grunt at the start of, or during, urination? Does he have a urinary stream that starts and stops rather than flowing consistently? Or a urinary stream that sprays? Or a

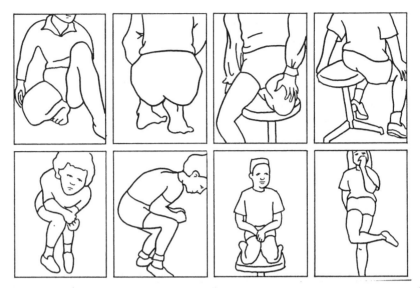

Figure 1.1. Signs of daytime urinary urgency. When children sense the sudden, urgent need to urinate, they may assume these body positions. After Kondo et al., "Holding Postures Characteristic of Unstable Bladder." Courtesy of the *Journal of Urology.*

straight, jetlike stream rather than a stream that forms an oval near the top when it exits?

Irritable erections. Does your son have frequent erections during the day? These are called irritable because they are due to internal inflammation and irritation rather than to arousal.

If you see that your child has any of these daytime symptoms or signs, you need to tell the doctor about them because they indicate the possibility of certain causes for the bedwetting, and they exclude others. For example, they indicate that the bedwetting may very likely be caused by a urethral obstruction, such as a narrowing or small fold, which causes the building of pressures and inflammations in the urethra. (Much more will be said about this and all of the other causes in later chapters.)

Or daytime symptoms indicate that another possible cause could be frequent constipation, involuntary bowel movements (*encopresis*), hemorrhoids, and/or inflammation (redness, soreness) around the anal or the genital area.

Daytime symptoms can also point to the possibility of a disease, such as diabetes. At the same time, the presence of daytime symptoms in most cases rules out a nighttime shortage of vasopressin as a cause.

When Daytime Symptoms Are Not Present

If you observe that your long-term bedwetter has none of the daytime symptoms described in the previous section, her bedwetting probably has other causes. For example, one of the most likely is a nighttime shortage of *vasopressin*, a naturally occurring hormone that limits production of urine. Other possibilities are very heavy sleep or sleep disturbances.

DOES MY CHILD WET BECAUSE OF A KIDNEY INFECTION?

Like many parents, you may fear that your child bedwets because of a kidney problem; however, doctors find that the vast majority of bedwetters have perfectly normal kidneys. Only rarely do they find kidney disease.

I found (as other physicians did) that in about 10 percent of the children who wet, X rays revealed an abnormal backing up of urine from the bladder to the kidneys. This condition is called *reflux*. If the bladder contains bacteria, reflux can lead to a kidney infection. Even if the bladder does not contain bacteria, the abnormal pressure of reflux may injure the kidneys. So, although kidney problems are not the likeliest cause of your child's bedwetting, they should certainly be investigated.

DOES MY CHILD WET BECAUSE OF URINARY INFECTIONS?

Although physicians always look carefully for urinary infections in children who bedwet, they rarely find them in boys. They do find them in about 20 percent to 30 percent of the girls who wet. These infections in girls result from the closeness of the urethral opening to the anal canal. The most common bacteria found in such infections is *E. coli*, which is the most common bacteria found in the stool.

However, as you will learn in later chapters, physical abnormalities in the urethra that cause long-term bedwetting also contribute to the development of infections. I believe that infections are rarely the true cause of long-term bedwetting, but rather are the result of the underlying condition. I have seen that when urethral problems are treated, both the bedwetting and the recurrent infections are relieved in most cases.

ARE THERE SOME THINGS THAT PROMOTE WETTING?

Many things can promote occasional wetting in normal children and can also aggravate the rate of wetting in enuretic children. Some of these things are illnesses, constipation, great fatigue, unusual anxiety, excessive intake of fluids (even overeating of watermelon), large doses of sedatives, and drugs to treat epilepsy or asthma. In addition, cold weather promotes more bedwetting than warm weather. (If your child wets more in cold weather, be sure she is warmly covered on cool nights.)

CAN OTHER CONDITIONS BE CONFUSED WITH BEDWETTING?

Two conditions are sometimes mistaken for bedwetting. Both are found only in girls.

In the first, the girl urinates normally on the toilet, but the urine strikes her labia in such a way that it ricochets into her vagina, where it pools. Later it dribbles out and wets her nightclothes or the bed. If your daughter is wetting the bed, but not with a large amount of urine, you may want to investigate this possibility. You will need to consult a urologist.

In the other condition, one of the ureters (tubes through which urine flows from the kidney to the bladder) ends abnormally in the vagina instead of the bladder. The result is a continual drip of urine. This condition is encountered only rarely, but it is important to be alert to it. If you suspect that your daughter's problem is a continual drip of urine, you should arrange for a urological examination for her.

One of my past patients, a married woman and mother of several children, was thought to be a bedwetter from early childhood until she entered my care. The situation caused her enormous grief. Through various tests and examinations, I found that one of her ureters descended abnormally from a partially diseased kidney into her vagina rather than into her bladder, causing a continual leakage of urine. After the diseased portion of the kidney and the useless ureter were removed, the leakage ended. How unfortunate that no doctor had recognized her particular symptoms much earlier in her life.

DO BEDWETTERS OUTGROW THEIR PROBLEM?

Your child may stop wetting as he grows older, even without treatment. The great majority of bedwetters stop gradually between ages eight and twelve. According to some researchers, about 15 percent of bedwetters stop by themselves each year. In general, you can expect an untreated child who wets at age five to continue to wet for three to seven more years. Most bedwetters who do not have daytime urinary symptoms stop sooner than bedwetters who do have daytime symptoms.

Many physicians mistakenly believe that the majority of enuretic children stop wetting simply because they outgrow their problem. It's true that some bedwetters who have no daytime symptoms may outgrow their bedwetting. However, in my experience, and in the experience of a number of other researchers, bedwetters carry the *underlying* physical problem into their adult lives. They may stop wetting as their sleep grows lighter and they awaken more easily, but, if left untreated, they will have to get up from one to three (or more) times a night to urinate, and they will continue to be burdened with their daytime symptoms. In addition, if they are male, their prostate glands may be affected, and their sexual lives may be painful. If they are female, they may experience frequent infections, and intercourse may become painful.

This is what happened with a 36-year-old businessman who came to me for help. He had wet the bed until age 16, and then had stopped wetting and thought he was cured. However, although he was no longer wetting his bed, he still had daytime urinary frequency, and a poor urinary stream. Later he had episodes of prostatitis, as well as painful and premature ejaculations. Irritable erections had troubled him so often that, to escape embarrassment, he had taped his penis to his lower abdomen and had constantly worn a jock strap. In addition, he could not get a night's sleep without having to get up three times to urinate.

I found that all of these problems were produced by the continued underlying cause of his earlier bedwetting: subtle folds in the back part of the urethra that partially blocked the flow of urine and caused the urethra to become inflamed. Following the simple treatment that cured him—removal of the subtle folds in the urethra—he was ecstatic! He no longer had to get up nights, nor be embarrassed by irritable erections, nor suffer painful and premature ejaculations. But how much better it would have been for him if the underlying causes had been diagnosed and treated when he was still a child.

Unfortunately, if your child's longtime bedwetting stops by itself (that is, without treatment), you can't assume that the underlying physical cause is cured. Continue to investigate the underlying cause, and, if necessary, obtain treatment for it.

WHAT HAPPENS IF BEDWETTING GOES UNTREATED?

One of the most serious results of letting the problem of bedwetting go untreated (as Harry C. Miller reported in the journal *Consultant*) is that overlooked physical abnormalities, even diseases, may grow worse as the bedwetter grows older.

I have seen adult enuretics who suffered with a variety of problems that could have been avoided if their bedwetting (and its underlying causes) had been treated in childhood.

A 45-year-old woman, for example, who had wet her bed until age 36, managed to awaken most nights to go to the bathroom, which she had to do three or four times a night. Over the years, she had suffered frequent urinary infections. Whenever she had one of these infections, or was developing a cold, or was very fatigued, she still experienced episodes of bedwetting. In addition, she needed to strain to urinate, and she wet her clothing somewhat during the day when she coughed, sneezed, or laughed. She needed to urinate very frequently. In her words, she "lived in the bathroom."

Upon examination, I found that the opening of her urethra (to the outside) was inadequate in size, and the lining of the urethra was inflamed because of this blockage. This constriction was responsible for her long years of bedwetting and worsening problems. After simple procedures were completed to enlarge the opening and treat the inflamed urethral lining, the woman's daytime symptoms disappeared. She then needed to get up only once each night to urinate; and in the 10 years since this cure, she has experienced only rare urinary infections. Had her bedwetting (and its underlying causes) been treated much earlier in life, she would have been spared years of problems, which only grew worse with the passage of time.

In addition to the physical problems that can result from untreated enuresis, wetting the bed can do great damage to your child's self-image and self-esteem. Unfortunately, bedwetters suffer shame, embarrassment, restriction of social activity, a terrible sense of helplessness, and sometimes even mental or physical abuse. Thus, untreated bedwetting causes some children to become passive, shy, and withdrawn, and causes others to become overly aggressive and combative. As the researchers Daniel S. Hellman and Nathan Blackman reported in the *American Journal of Psychiatry*, untreated, long-term bedwetting in childhood has been connected with pyromania (setting fires) and cruelty to animals. In adulthood it has been connected with violence, even murder. Most of these problems result from the mental and physical abuse that bedwetters experienced from their parents or other caregivers, siblings, or other children. Although in some families wetting does not seem to trouble the parents or the children, in the majority of families it leads to difficult parent-child conflict.

In a personal essay, the famous author George Orwell, who was a bedwetter, gives us a view of one childhood situation:

> In those days [bedwetting] was looked upon as a disgusting crime which a child committed on purpose and for which the proper cure was a beating. . . . Night after night I prayed, with a fervor never previously attained in my prayers, Please God, do not let me wet my bed! but it made remarkably little difference. Some nights the thing happened, others not. . . . Oh, the despair, the feeling of cruel injustice, after all my prayers and resolutions and once again waking between the clammy sheets.

After a particularly severe beating for bedwetting, Orwell remembers:

> I was crying partly because I felt this was expected of me, partly from genuine repentance, but partly also because of a deeper grief . . .: a sense of desolate loneliness and helplessness, of being locked up not only in a hostile world but in a world of

good and evil where the rules were such that it was actually impossible for me to keep them.

We can understand the connection that researchers make between long-term bedwetting and very antisocial behavior only when we learn of the abuse inflicted on children who wet the bed. For example, one of the murderers interviewed in prison by the author Truman Capote (for the book *In Cold Blood*) was a man who had been a bedwetter and had lived in orphanages and children's shelters as a child. For wetting the bed, he had been beaten savagely and punished so cruelly by caregivers that in one instance he nearly died.

Not only bedwetting, but also the daytime problems that many bedwetters experience (such as wetting one's clothing in school) disturb children far more than most adults realize.

Of course, some wetters overcome their problems and go on to rich, fulfilling lives as adults—as did Michael Landon, Sigmund Freud, Salvador Dali, James Joyce, and George Orwell. Some go on to become doctors. According to my own research—in which I questioned one hundred doctors—20 percent of doctors wet their beds in childhood. And at a meeting of urologists where the question "How many of you wet the bed in childhood?" was posed by the famous urologist Victor A. Politano, approximately 50 percent of the audience raised their hands!

It is important to remember that your child has no control over his bedwetting or daytime symptoms and needs treatment for the underlying physical causes.

DOES A BEDWETTER NEED AN EXAMINATION BY A PHYSICIAN?

All bedwetters need medical attention. Be sure to notice and to point out to your child's doctor any persistent symptoms or problems you observe.

First, the pediatrician or family doctor will need to take a medical history, do a physical examination, and take a urine sample for analysis. He should want to know whether your child shows daytime symptoms, and whether the wetting has continued from birth or started after a period of dryness of at least six months.

Among other things, this doctor will want to rule out certain diseases, such as diabetes, and look for easily observable problems, such as an overly small opening in the penis, redness or soreness around the genital or anal area, hemorrhoids, or worms. The doctor will want to question you about whether your child experiences sleep problems, chronic constipation, or allergies—any of which can cause or contribute to bedwetting. It is important to tell this doctor about every possible symptom, however unrelated to bedwetting it may seem, and to ask that all of the things mentioned here be looked for.

The pediatrician or family doctor can treat some of these conditions, but will refer you to the appropriate specialist for a cause he or she suspects but cannot treat.

ARE SOME TREATMENTS DANGEROUS AND/OR INEFFECTIVE?

You will need to be very careful in deciding on the best treatment for your child, because treatments offered by various health professionals still range from the ridiculous and harmful to the helpful and curative. In addition, many treatments that are offered are at odds with one another. Some doctors advise parents to awaken the child to go to the toilet; some advise against it. Some advise giving the wetter large quantities of water to drink; some advise withholding fluids. In the past, some doctors advised giving the child salt or very salty foods (such as salt herring) at the evening meal or at bedtime. (Regrettably, some parents are still doing that.)

It is important for you to be aware of the dangers in many of these "treatments." While you may safely lift your child out of bed to go to the toilet, you should never give him unusually large quantities of water, nor should you ever withhold a reasonable amount of fluid from him. Either of these "treatments" is abusive and could be harmful to your child's health. Withholding fluids, particularly during warm weather, or when your child has developed a fever, is especially dangerous because of the possibility of dehydration. It is also useless as well as dangerous to require a child to eat extra salt. Most children get far too much salt anyway, because of the salty snack foods they eat; excessive amounts of salt can cause severe health problems in children.

The actor Michael Landon, who wet his bed until age 12, remembered (in an interview for *Family Weekly*) that one doctor had put him on a diet of pickled herring, saltines, and no water before he went to bed.

Landon said, "For five months that was my bedtime diet, and all I got was damned thirsty! I nearly died."

Be wary of other conflicting "treatments" that are still suggested by doctors. Some of these may include requiring your child to urinate as often as possible during the day; to resist the impulse to urinate as long as possible in order to "stretch the bladder"; and to start and stop the urinary stream during urination in order to "strengthen the muscles" that retain urine. Such efforts would not only force your child to become unhealthily preoccupied with his process of voiding, but also would be useless and time-consuming. Worse, resisting the impulse to urinate may cause backup (reflux) of urine from the bladder to the kidneys, with possible damage to the kidneys.

Despite all of the evidence today that long-term bedwetting from birth is physical and not behavioral, some treatments that doctors suggest are still behavioral in nature. They require the child to "take responsibility" for becoming dry. Some require parents and therapists to give encouragement and rewards, such as gold stars or gifts. However, as you learned earlier and will see more clearly in later chapters, your child cannot control bedwetting through conscious will. Such efforts will only set your child up for failure and will provoke guilt and misery.

One last caution: Some treatments involve the use of drugs. One commonly prescribed drug for all types of bedwetting is Tofranil (imipramine hydrochloride). This drug does promote dryness, but, as the *Physician's Desk Reference* and a great deal of other medical literature show, it is dangerous because of its serious side effects, which could include skin conditions, insomnia, agitation, a lowering of the number of white blood cells, kidney damage, and even death. An overdose of Tofranil is deadly. I would discourage the use of it for your child, except for occasional sleepovers or camping trips. Any use of it, of course, should be exactly as prescribed by the physician for *your* child (dosages vary from child to child), and each dose should be given by the parent or other responsible adult. The medication should be kept in a safe place where none of your children can get to it themselves.

The most effective treatment for your child's bedwetting depends upon what is causing your child to bedwet. Only by treating the underlying cause can the problem be solved.

This chapter has provided you with an overview to help you put into perspective the detailed information in the chapters that follow. The remaining chapters will help you understand the many causes and treatments of bedwetting. They will assist you in your search for the true cause of your child's wetting and for the best treatment. Be sure to read every chapter, in consecutive order. In the meanwhile, please remember to remain supportive of, and sympathetic to, your bedwetting child as you learn how to help him become dry.

2

WHAT YOU NEED TO KNOW ABOUT YOUR CHILD'S URINARY SYSTEM

To understand many of the causes of bedwetting and methods of treatment that you will read about in later chapters, you need to know something about the anatomy of the urinary system and how the system functions.

There is no need for you to learn every detail; I will provide you with a brief, easy-to-understand description of the major parts of the urinary system and how they work together. This will help you understand how very small abnormalities, and even bowel problems, can affect your child's urinary system and produce bedwetting and daytime urinary symptoms.

HOW THE PARTS OF THE URINARY SYSTEM INTERACT

The *urinary tract* consists of the *kidneys*, *ureters*, *bladder*, and *urethra* (see figure 2.1), some small glands, and one large gland, the *prostate*. (Most people do not realize that the female, too, has a prostate, although it is much smaller than the male's. See figure 2.2.)

All the organs that hold or transport urine are composed of *smooth, involuntary muscle*. That is, when things are normal, this is the kind of muscle that works automatically without our conscious control and without making us aware of its workings. For example, we normally do not feel the contractions of the smooth muscles that push food along the

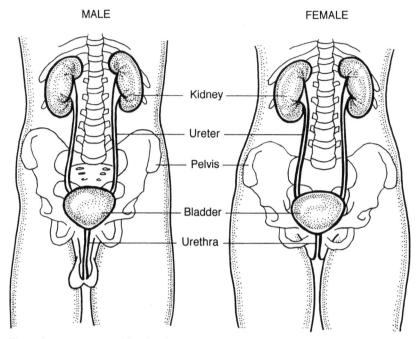

Figure 2.1.   The male and female urinary tracts.

intestines. The smooth, involuntary (automatic) muscles are different from the *striated* (nonsmooth), *voluntary* muscles, such as the ones we use when we throw a ball or run.

In addition to smooth muscles, the organs of the urinary tract have a smooth, delicate inner lining, like the lining of the mouth, and some rubber-bandlike elastic material that permits them to stretch. All urinary tract organs (like other organs in the body) contain blood vessels and nerves.

Kidneys and Ureters

The *kidneys*, which filter impurities out of the blood and produce urine, are fist-sized, bean-shaped organs about six inches long and three inches wide in adults, and proportionately smaller in children. They lie along the back wall of the abdominal cavity, on either side of the spine. The tubes that carry urine from the kidneys to the bladder are called the *ureters*. They are about 11 inches long and a quarter of an inch wide (about the width of a pencil) in adults, and proportionally shorter and thinner in

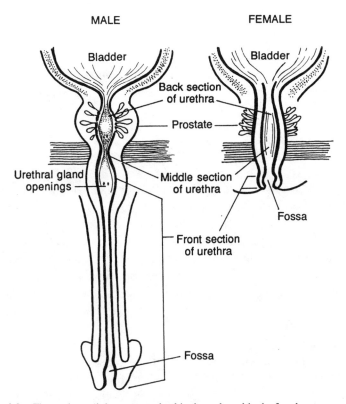

MALE   **FEMALE**

Bladder — Bladder
Back section of urethra
Prostate
Urethral gland openings — Middle section of urethra
Fossa
Front section of urethra
Fossa

Figure 2.2. The urethra and the prostate gland in the male and in the female.

children. One ureter descends from each kidney to the base of the bladder, which it enters from behind.

The Bladder

The *bladder* is a balloonlike muscular organ that acts as a storage area for urine and also as a pump. It relaxes to store urine and contracts to pump out or expel urine. In a newborn baby, the bladder holds only an ounce or two of urine, but by the time the baby is a year old, the bladder holds about four times as much. Normally, infants 3 to 6 months of age urinate about 20 times a day, and infants 6 to 12 months urinate about 16 times a day. At puberty, most youngsters reach the adult pattern of voiding: 4 to 6 urinations a day, approximately 8 to 10 ounces each. However, this varies widely from person to person.

The amount of urine a person passes at one time is not the full amount of urine the bladder can hold. Normally, people experience the first desire to urinate (or void) when the bladder contains about 5 to 7 ounces, but they don't usually urinate until it contains about 10 ounces. Even when a person feels an urgent need to void, the bladder can still hold more.

The Urethra

The *urethra* (see figure 2.2 again) is a tube or channel that carries urine from the bladder to the outside of the body, and it is a far more complex organ than the bladder. In both males and females, it discharges not only urine but also secretions of the prostate gland. In males, it also discharges semen. It contains within its walls the smooth, involuntary muscles that automatically contract to prevent urine from flowing out of the body when the bladder is storing urine. The same involuntary muscles automatically relax to allow urine to pass when the bladder is pumping out urine. The urethra also contains an enormous number of sexual, sensory, and pain nerve endings.

As the urethra comes away from the bladder, it contains three sections we will call the "back" section, the "middle" section, and the "front" section. The back section begins at the bladder opening (or bladder neck) and runs like a tunnel through the prostate gland. This section of the urethra in both male and female adults is a little over an inch long.

Inside the back part of the urethra, along the back wall, runs a narrow, streamlined ridge of tissue called a *crest* (see figure 2.3). It is prominent in the male and more subtle in the female. In both males and females, the crest begins just below the bladder opening, gradually forming a ridge or protrusion inside the back part of the urethra, and then growing smaller again until it splits into two strands and disappears into the middle section of the urethra. On each side of the crest runs a furrow. Ducts (channels) from the prostate empty into the furrow. By means of these ducts, the prostate gland sends its secretions into the urethra. In addition, in males, the middle of the crest forms a small, mound-shaped structure called the *verumontanum*, which contains two openings on its face. At the time of orgasm, semen is carried through ducts to these two openings, where the semen enters the urethra and is transported to the outside.

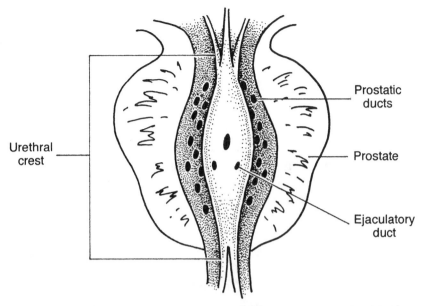

Figure 2.3. The urethral crest and prostate in the male. The crest is a narrow ridge of tissue on the floor of the back section of the urethra. It contains the openings of the ducts through which semen passes into the urethra. A furrow on each side of the crest contains many ducts through which secretions enter the urethra.

The middle section of the urethra in both males and females is less than half an inch long. It is surrounded by voluntary muscles (which will be described later).

After passing through these muscles, the male and female urethras differ a great deal (see figure 2.2 once more). In both males and females, the urethra passes through the pelvic floor. In the male, the front section extends several inches (through the length of the penis) and ends in a nozzlelike structure, where it opens to the outside. In the female, the urethra's front section consists only of the "nozzle," which is about one-third of an inch in length.

It is important to know that the urethra and bladder bear a close relationship to the anal canal and rectum (through which we pass our solid wastes). They all originate from one saclike structure in the pelvis of the developing embryo. As the embryo grows, a partition divides this sac into two parts: The part in front becomes the bladder and urethra, and the part behind becomes the anus and rectum. These structures contain branches from the same nerves and blood vessels (throughout the life of the individual). Knowing this, you can readily see why an abnormality in one area can affect the other.

The Prostate Gland

The prostate gland is a spongy structure about the size of a chestnut in the male but much flatter in the female. (The flat, less centralized prostate in the female resembles the prostate of a male child who has not yet reached puberty.) In the adult male, the prostate encircles the back section of the urethra like a collar around a horse's neck. In the female, it also surrounds the urethra, but much less prominently. The prostate gland contains numerous small ducts (channels) that carry prostatic secretions into the urethra. (See figure 2.3.) No one is certain what purpose this gland serves, and people can live very nicely without it.

Since people can live without a prostate, you may well wonder why we have one. The answer seems to be that it is an evolutionary vestige of the scent gland in animals. The scent gland evolved in animals as an aid to survival. Without sophisticated powers of scent and smell, most animals could not survive in the wilderness any more than humans could survive without their sight. Animals use scent and smell to mark out their territories, to tell friend from foe, to put down and follow trails, to detect prey, to avoid predators, and to attract sexual partners.

As the male animal makes his daily rounds, he periodically jets a squirt of urine containing the special scent *that comes from his prostate gland* on tree trunks, bushes, and other objects along his path. This spray of scent marks his territory, warns others to stay away from his territory, and also serves as an aromatic message to a female of his species, who may be responsive to it and may seek him out along his "marked" route.

Over the course of evolution, the sense of smell in humans has largely diminished or wasted away; it is extremely feeble in comparison with other animals' sense of smell. Human powers of smell are only about one-millionth as powerful as the dog's, for example, says the internationally renowned British science writer Elaine Morgan in her book *The Descent of Woman*. Still, humans continue to possess a prostate gland. The prominent urologist O. S. Lowsley reported in his book *Sexual Glands of the Male* that the prostate gland produces a "characteristic aromatic odor." Given this, we can safely suppose that the gland produces a sexual scent we no longer use.

Sphincters

Sphincters are muscles in and around the urethra that act as gates that open and close to control the flow of urine (see figure 2.4). These sphincters consist of two kinds of muscles: the *involuntary muscles* that work automatically, and the *voluntary muscles* that work under conscious control.

The smooth muscles in the bladder neck and the smooth muscles that make up the walls of the back and middle parts of the urethra are the internal, involuntary muscles.

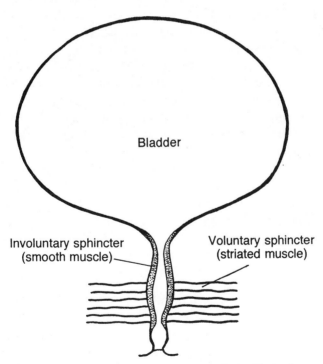

Figure 2.4. The sphincters: the muscles that prevent the loss of urine. The involuntary muscles of the bladder neck and back part of the urethra make up the internal sphincter. They work automatically. The voluntary muscles surrounding the urethra make up the external sphincter. They work under conscious control. The voluntary muscles assist the involuntary ones, but they cannot maintain control by themselves.

A group of striated muscles that surround the middle part of the urethra are the voluntary muscles. This group of muscles is called *the external sphincter*. Actually, there are two layers of muscles in the external sphincter. The voluntary muscles closest to the urethra contain "slow twitch" fibers, which react slowly but resist getting tired. The outer layer of the external sphincter contains "fast twitch" fibers, which react quickly but get tired rapidly. The slow-twitch group enables you to put off going to the toilet for a while, and the fast-twitch group enables you to stop urinating suddenly. You use the fast-twitch group during high-pressure conditions such as coughing, sneezing, lifting heavy weights, or any time you are in sudden danger of involuntarily losing some urine.

In addition to the internal and external sphincters, there is the large *pelvic floor*, which stretches across the pelvic cavity like a hammock and upon which the bladder and rectum rest. Although the pelvic floor is not actually a sphincter, it contains voluntary muscles that can help you prevent the exit of urine for a short period of time. When you contract the pelvic floor muscles, you raise the base of the bladder, which helps to close the bladder neck. The urethra and anal canal both pass through the pelvic floor muscles; the pelvic floor can help squeeze both of these canals, temporarily, to prevent involuntary loss of urine or stool. Conversely, when you relax the pelvic floor, urine can flow. In fact, a person who cannot relax this muscle properly cannot urinate properly, if at all.

Despite the roles played by your voluntary muscles, it is the bladder neck and urethra (involuntary muscle sphincters) that are the essential sphincters. Damage to these sphincters results in *incontinence* (no control over urination). Your voluntary muscles by themselves can stop the exit of urine only briefly and temporarily.

HOW THE URINARY TRACT WORKS

About 160 quarts of blood flow through your kidneys each day. The kidneys behave like very intelligent filters, filtering waste products out of the blood and producing urine to carry out the wastes, while sending substances that your body needs back to the blood. The ureters transport urine from the kidneys to the bladder. The urine enters the bladder and is stored there until voiding becomes necessary.

The Urinating Cycle

At first, the bladder collects urine without your awareness of it. As more urine fills the bladder, pressure increases in the bladder and inside the urethra (which tightens automatically as the bladder fills). Nerve endings (called "neuroreceptors") in the bladder send messages to part of the autonomic nervous system (the nervous system that works automatically); the nervous system in turn directs the bladder to remain relaxed to receive urine, and the urethra to remain tightened to prevent urination as the bladder continues filling. The slow-twitch fibers of the voluntary sphincter also tighten.

Normally, you may feel a mild need to urinate when the bladder contains 5 to 7 ounces of urine (less than a cupful). As the amount of urine increases, the pressure on the nerve endings in the bladder and in the urethral walls reaches a point where these nerve endings begin to send electrical signals to your brain telling you it is time to relieve yourself. (The sensation people experience when they say their bladders are full actually occurs mostly in the urethral and lower bladder areas. In fact, even if the bladder does not contain a drop of urine, pressure upon the back section of the urethra, such as the pressure of a catheter, makes people feel that they have to urinate.)

In response to the "need to urinate" signal, your brain sends electrical messages commanding the voluntary sphincters to tighten. Since you have done this all your life, you usually do not think about it, but it is actually a voluntary action. When you tighten the voluntary sphincter, you keep the bladder from emptying until you can reach the toilet. When you are ready, your brain commands the voluntary sphincters and the pelvic floor muscle to relax. Then the involuntary sphincters also relax; urine enters the urethra, and the voiding process begins. Nerve endings in the urethra that sense the passage of urine keep the urethra relaxed and keep the bladder contracting until the bladder empties. Then you contract or tighten up the voluntary muscles that surround the urethra to squeeze out any urine that remains in the urethra.

Urine Flow

Urine moving through the urethra flows like water running between the banks of a river. It follows the laws of fluid flow. Depending on conditions, the flow is gentle and smooth (laminar) or agitated and rough

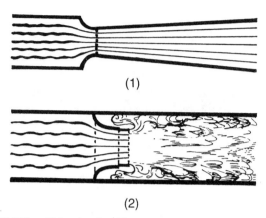

(1)

(2)

Figure 2.5.   Fluid flow. (1) Laminar flow: The stream is calm and smooth. (2) Turbulent flow: The stream is churning, rough, and agitated.

(turbulent). (See figure 2.5.) Inside the urethra, the flow of urine exerts a side pressure (called static pressure) against the walls of the urethra, and a forward-moving (or dynamic) pressure that keeps the stream flowing. You can understand what happens when urine flows through the urethra if you can visualize water flowing through a fireman's hose: The static (side) pressure changes the shape of the hose from flat to circular, and the moving, dynamic pressure drives the stream forward.

Some very important things happen when the inside of the channel is not of the same width from beginning to end, but instead is wider in some places and narrower in others. When the flow moves from a narrow area into a wider area, the speed of the flow lessens, but its side pressure increases; it tends to push the walls of the tube farther apart. On the other hand, when the stream moves from a wide area into a narrower area, the speed of the flow increases, but its side pressures drop; this causes suction—it tends to draw in the walls of the tube. (This is called Bernoulli's principle.)

The shape and size of the opening in the nozzle at the end of a hose or tube are very important. To a great extent, they determine the shape and force of the water that comes out of it. A wide-open nozzle produces a broad, gentle flow; a narrowed nozzle produces a narrow, high-power flow. The smaller the opening of the nozzle, the farther the stream will extend, as long as the system maintains its head of pressure. Anyone who has adjusted the nozzle of a garden hose while keeping the faucet at the same setting is familiar with the results of wider and narrower openings.

How do these facts apply to the urinary system? When you urinate, urine in the bladder moves slowly, with a high static (side) pressure. The urine enters the narrow back section of the urethra (which is made even narrower by the urethral crest), and moves rapidly, with a low or negative static (side) pressure, creating suction. As I showed in a 1974 article I coauthored with Arthur Ginsburg and Arthur Babson, since the prostate gland makes secretions that we find in the voided urine, this drop in static pressure may actually suction the secretions into the urinary stream. In the male, when the stream reaches the wide front part of the urethra, it slows, but its side pressure increases. The increased side pressure pushes open the walls of the front section of the urethra, which has little if any muscle, and could not open by itself; and the stream is able to exit. In the female, the urine moves rapidly, with a low static pressure, through the much shorter female urethra. (In the female, you remember, the front part of the urethra consists only of the nozzle.) The forward-moving pressure carries the stream forward and out. In both the male and the female the size and shape of the nozzle determine the shape and speed of the exiting stream. It is easier to see this in boys than in girls, but the shape and speed of the exiting stream can let the doctor know whether the voiding pressure is normal or too high, and whether there may be an obstruction in the urethra. For example, a stream that flares before growing thinner again usually indicates normal conditions. A stream that is very rapid and straight—with no flare—indicates that there may be an abnormal narrowing in the urethra.

What does all this business of channels, pressures, and nozzles have to do with bedwetting? Actually, quite a bit.

WHAT HAPPENS WHEN THE URINARY SYSTEM DOESN'T WORK AS IT SHOULD?

The bladder, the urethra, and the urinary flow exist in a very delicate balance that is easily upset. In a person with inflammation of the bladder (cystitis), for example, the bladder contracts with abnormal pressure and drives urine into the urethra faster than the urethra can handle it. Also, a tiny fraction of an inch change in the opening of the urethra, a tiny constriction or obstruction somewhere within the length of the urethra, a slight weakening and stretching of urethral walls, or a patch of roughness in the urethral lining can change a normal flow into an abnormal one.

Abnormal flows cause a number of serious but often overlooked problems. High-speed and turbulent flows injure the delicate linings of the urethra. Abnormal side pressure can block secretions from the prostate (causing it to swell), or it can even drive urine and infection-causing bacteria into the gland. And of greatest importance, abnormal pressure can force apart and weaken the sphincters (muscles) that prevent loss of urine (see figure 2.6). In addition, nerves irritated by these abnormal pressures can begin to behave like a hair trigger on a gun; abnormal pressures on nerve endings can make the urethra relax and the bladder contract before they should, which cause urination. Abnormal actions of

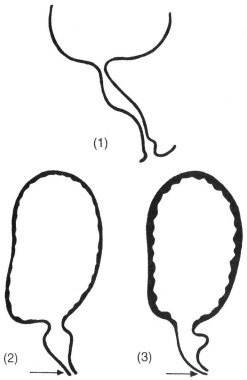

Figure 2.6. The effects of urethral obstruction. Outlines traced from X-ray photos show (1) a normal bladder and urethra and (2) and (3) abnormal ones. Arrows point to the areas of urethral obstruction. Pressures behind the obstruction pushed apart and weakened the muscles of the urethral walls. (These muscles need to remain strong to prevent the loss of urine.)

the urethral system can range from the hardly noticed to the painfully obvious.

Even the smallest disturbance in the normal workings of your body can cause trouble. Consider the "something" you get in your eye now and then, the ingrown toenail, or the infected tooth, and the ways in which these things affect you. No wonder, then, that subtle constrictions, inflammations, and other physical factors affect the processes of the lower urinary tract and cause loss of control.

This overview of the urinary system will help you to understand material in several chapters, especially those that explain how urethral abnormalities, chronic constipation, inflammations, and allergic reactions can contribute to bedwetting and can be treated.

3

SLEEP FACTORS THAT CONTRIBUTE TO BEDWETTING

Is your bedwetting child, like the majority of bedwetters, almost impossible to awaken? Although heavy sleep is sometimes the principal cause of bedwetting, most often it is a contributor to bedwetting, no matter what the central cause. Therefore, it is important for you to gain an understanding of the role this arousal disorder plays in your child's bedwetting. In addition to the heaviness of sleep, other sleep factors may play a role in bedwetting.

THE ROLE OF HEAVY SLEEP
IN BEDWETTING

Parents of a large majority of the bedwetters I have treated described these children as extremely heavy sleepers, much more difficult to awaken than their nonwetting children. They reported that their bedwetters are unaffected by thunder and lightning, police sirens, vacuum-cleaner noise, alarm systems designed to awaken bedwetters, physical prodding, and even falling out of bed! One doctor told me about his own enuretic son who fell out of the top level of a set of bunk beds: The boy fractured his wrist, but remained asleep until the next morning!

So it is not unusual for parents to speak of the bedwetting child's sleep as "the sleep of the dead." Of the more than three thousand bedwetters my medical partner and I treated, the parents of approximately 90 percent claimed that their children who wet the bed were extremely difficult or nearly impossible to arouse from sleep. These children suffer from an arousal disorder that causes them to sleep through such urgent promptings and stimuli as the need to urinate. At the same time, we learned that children who also have urinary problems (such as the need to urinate frequently and with immediate urgency), but who sleep lightly, awaken to go to the toilet at night—sometimes many times each night.

In one of my early studies, I divided 450 children who had urinary problems into two groups. In Group 1 were 300 children who had both daytime and nighttime problems—they had daytime urinary frequency and urgency, and they also wet their beds. In Group 2 were 150 children who had the same daytime urinary symptoms but did not wet their beds. Then I asked the parents about the heaviness of their children's sleep. Parents described 90 percent of children in Group 1 (bedwetters) as very *heavy* sleepers; these children did not awaken to urinate. Parents described 80 percent of the children in Group 2 (*nonbedwetters*) as *light* sleepers; these children awakened at night to urinate.

My findings are similar to those published in *Acta Paediatrica* by the Danish researcher Søren Wille, who asked a large group of parents to awaken their children at 5:00 A.M. Based on the parents' reports, about 75 percent of bedwetters were difficult (almost impossible) to arouse, in contrast with 7 percent of the nonwetters.

Although we know that this arousal disorder afflicts the majority of bedwetters (those with daytime symptoms as well as those without them), we do not yet know what causes it.

Four Stages of Sleep

The knowledge we have about the stages of sleep offers some clues about the role of heavy sleep in bedwetting.

With the use of electrical instruments that measure brain activity, muscle cell activity, and eye movements—along with instruments that measure bladder pressure, blood pressure, pulse, and breathing rates— scientists have developed the following "EEG (electroencephalographic) picture" of sleep and its relationship to bedwetting.

Sleep consists of two major parts. One is a period in which most dreaming occurs; this is characterized by rapid eye movements (REM) and is called "REM sleep." The other part is "non-REM sleep," a period in which there is little dreaming and no rapid eye movements. Non-

REM sleep is further divided into sleep stages 2, 3, and 4. Researchers such as the eminent Roger J. Broughton consider stages 3 and 4 to be "deep sleep," because during these periods heart and breathing rates, muscle tone, and mental activity appear to be at their lowest levels. The four stages repeat themselves in cycles a number of times each night.

According to researcher Howard P. Roffwarg and his associates, young children spend more time in deep sleep stages 3 and 4 than older children do. That means that as children grow older, they spend less time in deep sleep stages 3 and 4, but more time in stages 1 and 2, when they can awaken more easily. (This fact may help to explain why fewer children bedwet as they grow older, even though they may have other underlying causes that remain with them.)

Brain wave patterns recorded on EEGs indicate that, as the sleep cycles repeat themselves through the night, the sleep depth of all four stages grows lighter, and the child may become somewhat easier to awaken in the later cycles. However, as researchers Charles H. Best and Norman B. Taylor reported in their book *The Physiological Basis of Medical Practice*, some youngsters may descend briefly into a deeper sleep just before morning. These facts may account for the findings that, although children can wet during any sleep stage, they wet most often during the first third of the night (when sleep is deepest), and some wet again just before morning (when, for them, there is another period of deep sleep).

Another interesting thing about sleep is that *all* the stages of sleep grow lighter as we grow older, and so, as we age, we awaken more easily from any sleep stage.

A few researchers believe that the sleep of bedwetting children does not differ from the sleep of nonbedwetters. However, in my considerable clinical experience, as well in as the experience and research of many others (including the recent report by Søren Wille mentioned earlier in this chapter), the evidence of heavy sleep in bedwetters is very strong. Whether you call it "heavy sleep," "deep sleep," or "an arousal disorder"—as various researchers do—the majority of bedwetters are much more difficult to arouse than most children who do not wet their beds.

How Heavy Sleep Contributes to Bedwetting

Sleep relaxes the voluntary muscles, which are the muscles we use for deliberate movements, such as throwing a ball or walking. Some voluntary muscles that relax during sleep are the ones we use to hold urine back briefly, until we can get to a toilet. If your child is a heavy sleeper, these voluntary muscles are of no help to him.

At the same time, sleep does *not* relax involuntary muscles, such as the involuntary muscles in the intestines, the ureters, the urethra, and the bladder. They keep on working. When the involuntary muscles of the urethra relax and those of the bladder contract, the bladder expels urine. In fact, researchers Henri Gastaut and Roger J. Broughton reported in the book *Recent Advances in Biological Psychiatry* that bladder pressure and bladder contractions *increase* among some bedwetters as sleep deepens. If your child is a heavy sleeper, she has no control over these involuntary contractions, which lead to bedwetting.

Dreams Do Not Cause Bedwetting

Some people (including doctors) used to believe that a dream that occurs during sleep causes a child to wet the bed, but that theory is no longer thought to be true.

According to Gastaut and Broughton, the wetting episode generally begins with an increase in bladder contractions, body movements, and heart and breathing rates during nondreaming sleep. As the bladder empties, sleep lightens, at times to momentary awakening. After urination, the sleeper falls back rapidly to the depth of sleep he was in before the wetting took place. Awakening a child right after a bedwetting episode requires considerable effort. Unlike nonwetters, when wetters are awakened they react sluggishly to light shined in their eyes. They also show confusion, disorientation, and a lack of awareness that they lie in a wet bed. Generally, they report no dreams at that time.

Later the children often report dreams in which they have urinated in a bathroom or some other suitable place. However, according to researchers, these dreams do not occur during the actual wetting episode; they occur later, when sleep lightens. As the children move into the lighter, dreaming phase of sleep, they sense the wetness of the sheets and dream they are urinating in the bathroom. In fact, if the wet sheets are removed right after the urination, these dreams do not occur at all.

It is interesting that when bedwetters awaken to a dry bed they believe, absolutely, that they did not wet, and they will argue you into the ground about it. They have total amnesia about the episode!

VASOPRESSIN SHORTAGE DURING SOME CHILDREN'S SLEEP

In sleep, the kidneys continue to produce urine, but normally a hormone called vasopressin causes the kidneys to produce less urine at night than during the day. Unfortunately, as many researchers—such as Marie Birkasova and her associates (in the journal *Pediatrics*)—have shown, a significant number of bedwetters have a shortage of this hormone. Such children produce about four times more urine at night than the bladder can hold. Thus, the shortage of vasopressin, which is probably genetic (inherited), in combination with heavy sleep, results in a great deal of bedwetting. (The shortage of vasopressin and the treatment for it will be discussed fully in chapter 8.)

SLEEPWALKING, NIGHT TERRORS, AND BEDWETTING

In their sleep pattern and in other ways, bedwetters have a great deal in common with children who sleepwalk and children who experience night terrors. Each of these conditions is associated with great difficulty in the ability to be aroused from sleep and is called a "sleep disturbance" by researchers. Each occurs most often in the early part of the night, during nondreaming sleep. When the children are awakened they show confusion and have minimal or no recall of the event.

Bedwetting, sleepwalking, and night terrors run in families; often two or all three conditions run in the same family. In fact, sleepwalkers are four times more likely than nonsleepwalkers to have a family history of bedwetting. And bedwetters sleepwalk more than nonwetters. Children generally grow out of these conditions by late adolescence. Researchers such as Roger J. Broughton and, more recently, Anthony Kales believe that there is an underlying relationship.

It is important to remember that in sleepwalking, night terrors, and bedwetting associated with arousal disorders, children cannot control their unusually heavy sleep no matter how strongly they may wish to control it.

It is possible that some sleepwalkers may even be looking for the bathroom. The evidence is anecdotal but interesting. A number of parents described to me how their sleepwalking bedwetters walked to wastebaskets, hampers, and corners of rooms, where they then urinated, still asleep. In addition, Gastaut and Broughton, working with sleepwalkers, induced attacks of sleepwalking by making their subjects drink large amounts of water before going to sleep, and then arousing them suddenly from deep sleep. The subjects then walked about, usually to a distant bathroom, and then returned to bed. After the episode, when the researchers awakened them again, the sleepwalkers had no memory of the event.

TREATING BEDWETTING CAUSED BY HEAVY SLEEP

Excessively heavy sleep is a contributing factor rather than a primary cause in most bedwetting, but in some cases it is the principal cause.

How can you treat your child's bedwetting if it is caused solely by heavy sleep and not by any other underlying physical problem?

For a time, physicians tried to treat the problem with drugs to lighten sleep, but they discontinued this approach. In addition to producing questionable results, the drugs caused unwanted side effects and were thought to be addictive.

The most practical solution at this time may be a wetness alarm or a wetness vibrator system (which you can purchase in a pharmacy, medical supply store, or department store, or you can order through a mail-order catalog). These systems are available with a number of different features, but they all operate on the same general principle. Some consist of a special pad; a source of current (battery); and an alarm bell, hooter, or vibrator. Others consist of a small sensor (with a buzzer or vibrator), which is attached to the child's underwear at night. Some of the most popular systems are called Potty Pager, Starry Night, and Night Train'r. (See figure 3.1 for some popular types.)

You place the pad under your child or attach the sensor to your child's underclothes; when wetting begins, the circuit closes and sets off the noise or vibration. It is hoped that your child will awaken and stop urinating, shut off the system, go to the bathroom to urinate, change his nightclothes, return to bed, and reset the device. In one to six months he may get through the night without bedwetting.

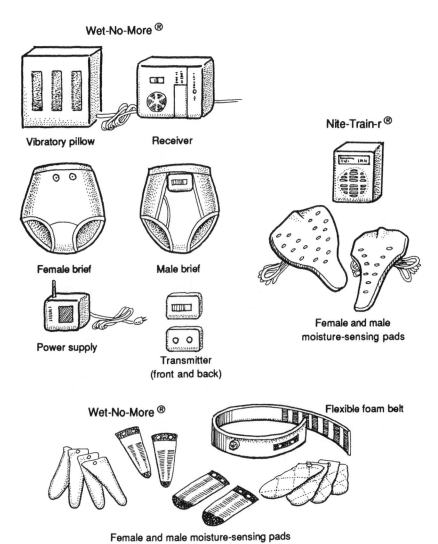

Figure 3.1.   Some popular types of wetness alarms. Reprinted by permission of Travis International Inc.

Among children who have no disease and no other underlying cause of wetting and who use the wetness alarm or vibrator system consistently, about 70 percent stop bedwetting. About 40 percent begin wetting again, but if the system is used again for a second course of treatment, the majority of these children eventually stop bedwetting.

No one knows exactly why the wetness alarm system works, and its discovery was accidental. Originally it was an alarm device introduced in a sanitarium to let the nurses know when children wet the bed and needed a change of bedclothes. Dr. Meinhard Pfaundler, the pediatrician at the institution, was surprised to find that with the use of the apparatus there was a gradual but very significant decrease in the number of bedwettings.

Unfortunately, the wetness alarm system has its drawbacks. It is generally safe, but there have been occasional reports of "cold burns" or irritations that have resulted with its use. Also, the sensor may become wet with sweat and set off the alarm at the wrong time. It may awaken other members of your family. Worst of all, it may fail to awaken your bedwetter, so that someone else has to turn the alarm off, and the bedwetter receives no help from the device. However, because of its success rate, it is worth trying.

Modern wetness alarm systems are smaller and neater than the older ones and are inexpensive. However, some systems are offered as part of a program that involves personal instruction and supervision by a professional; these programs are often expensive, and you must be cautious about the background and training of the "professional" who operates the program.

It is important to keep in mind that most persistent bedwetting is not caused solely by heavy sleep. Usually, heavy sleep is a contributing factor, but the principal cause is a small urological abnormality, a shortage of vasopressin, chronic constipation, or in a small number of cases, a food intolerance, or a condition such as diabetes, sickle-cell anemia, kidney disease, or pinworms. It is extremely important for you to obtain treatment and resolution of any underlying abnormality, shortage, intolerance, or disease rather than to mask the bedwetting symptom with a wetness alarm conditioning system. (And, of course, the wetness alarm system does nothing for the daytime urinary problems or damage that the underlying condition may be causing.)

For the majority of children, treatment of the principal cause, without an alarm system, cures or controls the bedwetting. For a smaller number of children, a wetness alarm may provide further help after the principal cause has been treated. For children whose wetting is caused solely by a sleep problem, the alarm is the safest, most effective treatment at present.

4

RULE OUT DISEASES EARLY

A number of different diseases and disorders can cause or contribute to bedwetting. Some of them cause wetting after a child has already been dry for at least six to twelve months (secondary wetting), although some of them cause wetting from birth (primary wetting). Among the diseases are diabetes mellitus, diabetes insipidus, hyperthyroidism (overactive thyroid), sickle-cell anemia, kidney ailments, nervous system diseases, and hyperactivity/attention deficit disorder. Although they are rare and the cause of bedwetting in only very few children, they are the first possibilities you should investigate and most probably rule out for your child.

On the slim chance that your child is one of the few who may be bedwetting because of one of these diseases, this chapter will describe the symptoms so that you can recognize them and bring them to the attention of your doctor. (Under any circumstances, be sure to ask your child's pediatrician or family doctor to check for them.) A physician's care, of course, is needed for any of these diseases or conditions.

This chapter will also alert you to some medications that can cause your child to wet the bed.

DIABETES MELLITUS

Diabetes mellitus, often called "sugar diabetes," is a disease most people know something about. "Diabetes" means "a siphoning off" or "a running through"; it describes a condition in which the body excretes a great deal of urine. "Mellitus" means "sweet" (containing sugar).

There are two types of diabetes mellitus. Physicians refer to type I, or insulin-dependent diabetes, which usually begins in youth but sometimes begins in adulthood; and type II, or insulin-independent diabetes, which generally begins after age 40, but sometimes begins in youth.

In type I, something unknown—perhaps a virus or injury—causes the destruction of special cells in the pancreas that normally produce a substance called *insulin*. Since insulin is responsible for regulating the amount of sugar in the blood, a lack of insulin permits blood sugar to build up to dangerous levels. The abnormal amount of sugar that builds up in the blood draws fluid (in a process of osmosis) from the tissues of the body into the bloodstream. In turn, the kidneys begin filtering out the sugar, and excreting it, along with the abnormally large quantities of fluid (urine) that have been drawn into the blood.

What are the symptoms? Children with type I diabetes have to run to the bathroom frequently; at the same time, they are often thirsty, and they drink a great deal. They complain of being tired, and they seem weak. Many lose weight. Some experience blurring of vision. Because resistance to infection is reduced, these children suffer more infections than other children. Girls, for example, may develop vaginal fungus infections. In addition, because of the large output of urine—and perhaps because a toxic effect of the disease on sleep makes awakening difficult—the child may begin wetting the bed even if she had been dry for years. In young children (aged approximately 7 to 10 years), the onset of bedwetting may be one of the early signs of diabetes.

It is very important that you bring to the doctor's attention any symptoms of diabetes in your child.

If your child has diabetes, the physician will place him on a special diet and prescribe carefully monitored doses of insulin. Your child will resume a relatively normal life. The bedwetting, too, will subside (unless there are additional, unrelated physical problems). The doctor most qualified to treat your child's diabetes is a pediatric endocrinologist. However, a pediatrician or even a family doctor also can treat this disease.

Type II diabetes mellitus is the type that seldom occurs in childhood. In type II, the pancreas produces insulin, but the body does not utilize it properly. The patient stores fat and gains weight. Otherwise, her symptoms are similar to those in type I. Type II cannot be treated with insulin because the body will not utilize it. Treatment, which must be under the care of a doctor, consists of rigorous exercise, a special diet, and loss of all excess weight.

Note: You must not withhold fluid from a child who is putting out a great deal of urine, because withholding fluid in any of these diabetic conditions can lead quickly to dangerous dehydration. Instead, your child should be seen by a doctor as soon as possible.

DIABETES INSIPIDUS

Diabetes insipidus (a disease that has nothing to do with sugar or the pancreas) is very, very rare in children. It has a number of causes. One is an injury or tumor in the area of the brain that normally produces the hormone vasopressin, which regulates the production of urine; the injury causes the brain to stop producing the hormone during both daytime and nighttime. Another cause is radiation or brain surgery performed to remove a tumor in the brain. Still another cause is a disease or injury to the kidneys that prevents the kidneys from responding to vasopressin.

Vasopressin controls the amount of fluid sent to the bladder by the kidneys. Produced in the posterior lobe of the pituitary gland, vasopressin normally travels through the bloodstream to the kidneys. There it directs the kidneys to reabsorb some of the water that is being sent to them, and to return this water to the bloodstream in order to maintain the proper concentration of blood and body fluids. If vasopressin is either not being produced in the pituitary gland or not being utilized by the kidneys, the amount of dilute fluid sent to the bladder is enormous—5 to 15 quarts or more in a 24-hour period.

Children who have diabetes insipidus are constantly thirsty, forever drinking, and often running to the bathroom to pass large quantities of almost colorless urine. Their hands may be very dry, and they may suffer constipation. If they sleep very lightly, they awaken many times during the night to urinate and to drink water; if they sleep heavily, they wet the bed. If your child shows these symptoms, be sure to tell his doctor about them. Until he receives treatment, he must be permitted to drink as much water as he feels he needs.

For a child whose pituitary gland is not producing sufficient vasopressin, a pediatric endocrinologist can prescribe the correct dose of the synthetic hormone desmopressin (DDAVP, Stimate, or a generic brand), which controls the problem very effectively. If an injury, surgery, or radiation to the brain is causing the problem, the gland may return to normal within a year. If a tumor is causing the problem, it will have to be removed.

In a child whose kidneys are the problem (because they cannot respond to vasopressin), the kidney specialist must treat the underlying kidney disease or injury. Desmopressin will not help this child.

Note: The physician must distinguish carefully between diabetes insipidus and another condition called *primary polydypsia*, which means compulsive drinking. Researchers think that primary polydypsia, a very rare condition, may result from a disorder in the thirst mechanism. Primary polydypsia should not be treated with desmopressin because, in this disease, the hormone will cause the child to retain fluid and "drown" in it (water intoxication).

HYPERTHYROIDISM (OVERACTIVE THYROID GLAND)

The thyroid gland, located just in front of the windpipe, produces the hormone *thyroxin*, which does many important things in the body: It helps to convert food to energy, maintain body temperature, and regulate growth. A number of problems can cause the gland to produce too much thyroxin, thus speeding up all of the body's chemical reactions and affecting both physical and mental processes. This condition is very rare in children, but researchers such as R. Goswami and associates, G. A. Kozeny and W. S. Wood, and S. S. Stoffer have found that where it occurs it can produce bedwetting.

The symptoms vary among individuals, but they include at least some of the following: fidgety behavior and hyperactivity (some parents may mistake this for hyperactivity/attention deficit disorder); emotional instability, nervousness, anxiety; poor sleep, inability to relax; tremor; rapid heartbeat, and palpitations. Symptoms may also include large appetite and a great deal of eating without weight gain (and possibly with weight loss); attacks of diarrhea, frequent loose stools; insensitivity to cold, intolerance to heat, increased sweating; weakness, breathlessness after physical activity; and bulging eyes.

If your child has a number of these symptoms, tell her physician. If tests show the presence of this condition, be sure that your child is referred to a pediatric endocrinologist who can discuss a number of possible treatments with you and choose knowledgeably from among them. Treatment for the overactive thyroid will also resolve the bedwetting.

SICKLE-CELL ANEMIA

Many children who have sickle-cell anemia wet their beds. In 1995, T. Ernesto Figueroa and a group of researchers at the South Florida Health Sciences Center found that about 30 percent of the center's 91 children who had sickle-cell disease had been wetting the bed since infancy.

Sickle-cell anemia is an inherited disease of the red blood cells. For years people thought that the disease occurred only in people of black African descent, but we know now that it also occurs in other groups, including people from parts of Italy, Greece, India, Arabia, and elsewhere.

Sickle-cell anemia begins early in life. Symptoms in about half of its victims start showing between the ages of six months and two years. In others, symptoms start showing later.

What is this disease? In a person with sickle-cell anemia, the hemoglobin (oxygen-carrying substance in the red blood cells) is defective; it does not get enough oxygen. This causes its molecules to combine with each other in a process called "polymerization." The red blood cells lose their flexibility to the point of becoming rigid, and, instead of round, they become sickle-shaped. A round shape permits easy flow, but the sickle shape, together with the rigidity, causes the red blood cells to clump together and block the flow of blood in the small blood vessels. The tissues that are normally supplied by the blocked vessels are damaged or destroyed because they are cut off from the oxygen and nutrients normally carried by the bloodstream. The process causes weakness and a great deal of pain. Any child with sickle-cell anemia needs the care of a physician.

In virtually all cases, the disease destroys the ability of the kidneys to concentrate urine, and the output of urine becomes greater than normal. The individual must awaken at night to urinate or wet the bed. (D. R. Readett reported that parents of sickle-cell children who bedwet consider these children more difficult to awaken than sickle-cell children who don't bedwet.)

What symptoms alert you to the presence of this disease? Among the earliest is swelling of the fingers and toes, then thickening of the bones of the hands and feet. The symptoms of anemia are present: paleness, weakness, fatigue, fainting, shortness of breath, and palpitations of the heart (when the heart tries to compensate for the anemia by pumping blood faster than normal).

A child with sickle-cell anemia is small for his age, and several times a year endures "sickle-cell crises," periods of severe pain in the abdomen, bones, joints, or muscles, accompanied by fever. These crises often require hospitalization.

Although there is still no cure, if your child suffers from this disease, the pain and other related problems can be treated. Blood transfusions and various drugs are used. You may want to inquire about hydroxyurea, a substance that was reported by a number of researchers, including S. Charache at Johns Hopkins School of Medicine, to be helpful in reducing the frequency of sickle-cell crises.

You can ask your child's physician to try giving the synthetic hormone desmopressin to control your child's bedwetting. In 1995, T. Ernesto Figueroa and his associates (mentioned earlier in this section) reported in the *Journal of Urology* that they gave desmopressin to 10 children with sickle-cell anemia, and six of them experienced a complete or partial relief from bedwetting.

And you may wish to look into the possibility of bone marrow transplant. A. Ferster and a group of researchers in Belgium reported in the *British Journal of Haematology* on the curative effects of bone marrow transplants in five children who had severe forms of the disease. Another researcher, Y. Beuzard, reported in 1992 in the French journal *Revue du Practicien* that bone marrow transplants had cured 30 patients.

There is still hope for a significant cure: At least one biotechnical company is working on the development of a gene therapy for sickle-cell anemia.

An additional note: If your child has sickle-cell anemia and daytime symptoms of urinary urgency in addition to nighttime frequency or bedwetting, then, besides other measures, you may want to ask the doctor to look for other possible urinary problems as well. Your child may have a urinary problem that is separate from the disease (as was the case with one of the children I treated).

KIDNEY DISEASE

Any disease or disorder that weakens or destroys the ability of the kidneys to concentrate the urine and return water to the bloodstream leads to the excretion of so much dilute urine that it is too much for the capacity of the bladder.

Any person with such a condition must urinate very frequently, and must awaken often at night to urinate. A child who does not sleep lightly wets the bed.

If your child urinates very frequently, she needs to be seen by a physician who can rule out other conditions. If the physician suspects kidney disease, he will refer your child to a urologist or to a kidney specialist who will perform the necessary examinations and tests. If a disease of the kidneys is discovered, the treatment will depend on the type of disease that is found.

NERVOUS SYSTEM DISORDERS

Any condition or injury that affects the brain or the nerves going to and from the bladder and urinary sphincters can lead to bedwetting. One example, which exists from birth, is *spina bifida*, a condition in which the spinal canal fails to close completely, thus leaving a cleft or defect. The condition almost always occurs on the low back. Often it is so subtle or hidden that it escapes detection except by X-ray examination; however, dimpling of the skin, an abnormal tuft of hair, or a small collection of fat under the skin in the lower area of the spine may give a clue to its existence. The hidden form of spina bifida has no symptoms, and exists in more than 50 percent of normal children.

In more obvious cases of spina bifida, the spinal cord and nerve roots bulge through the defect; they appear as a soft lump the size of a golf ball or a tennis ball in the lower back. This results in injury to the nervous tissue—with loss of urinary and bowel control, as well as loss of sensation in the pelvic area, and in some cases, paralysis of the legs. The severity of the symptoms depends on the severity of the nerve damage. Early surgical closing of the defect reduces the mortality and decreases the incidence of paralysis.

Your child's doctor would have already made you aware of spina bifida if your child had this condition in a form serious enough to cause bedwetting. Nevertheless, I include it here on the very slim chance that the doctor may have overlooked it.

Another very rare nervous system condition that can sometimes result in bedwetting is called *tethered cord*. In this condition, the tail end of the spinal cord becomes fixed to the surrounding tissue and cannot move up normally as the child grows. The stretching of the cord and dislocation of the nerve roots can lead to symptoms you would find with spina bifida. Some reports indicate that freeing the cord surgically from its attachments may lessen bedwetting and other symptoms, such as some loss of sensation, difficulty in walking, and paralysis.

A neurologist is the specialist who diagnoses and treats disorders of the nervous system.

HYPERACTIVITY/ATTENTION DEFICIT DISORDER

Although there is controversy about the causes, researchers agree that hyperactivity/attention deficit disorder (H/ADD) is not caused by psychological factors, and doctors and parents agree that many children with H/ADD wet their beds at night and wet themselves during the day. A study by researchers M. Bhatia and colleagues, published in the *Journal of Child Psychology and Psychiatry*, found that 29 percent of H/ADD children bedwet, compared to 5 percent of non-H/ADD controls. And a research group led by Joseph Biederman reported in the same journal that 32 percent of H/ADD children were bedwetters, as opposed to 14 percent of controls. A study of hyperactive boys by Anjana Sharma and colleagues (published in the *Indian Journal of Clinical Psychology*) also found that significantly more hyperactive children wet their beds than do other children. E. Ornitz and colleagues report that these children bedwet from birth (primary bedwetting).

According to John F. Taylor, in his book *Helping Your Hyperactive Child*, treating your child's hyperactivity disorder will also control the daytime and nighttime enuresis.

A study by J. Egger and colleagues, published in *Clinical Pediatrics*, found that eliminating certain foods and chemicals from the diets of H/ADD children eliminates or lessens their disorder and bedwetting. This study corroborates earlier studies by others.

If your bedwetting child has been diagnosed as having H/ADD and is not yet being treated for it, you may want to consult a physician as early as possible about appropriate treatment, not only to control the bedwetting but also to make a great difference in your child's life and in the life of the family.

If your child has not been diagnosed with this disorder but you strongly suspect that he may be suffering with it, take the steps to have him tested. You can ask your child's doctor or the school psychologist in your school district to recommend an appropriate medical professional to test your child.

Hyperactivity/attention deficit disorder is a very complicated subject. It cannot be addressed adequately in this chapter, but you can consult the following excellent books:

Helping Your Hyperactive Child by John F. Taylor, Ph.D. (Prima Publishing & Communications).

Is This Your Child? by Doris J. Rapp, M.D. (William Morrow & Company).

Is This Your Child's World? by Doris J. Rapp, M.D. (William Morrow & Company).

BEDWETTING CAUSED BY MEDICATIONS USED TO CONTROL DISEASES

Epilepsy Medication

Some people believe that epilepsy causes bedwetting, but it does not. However, drugs that treat epilepsy can cause bedwetting. If your child is epileptic and wets the bed, discuss the problem with the doctor who is treating the epilepsy.

Asthma/Allergy Medication

M. Eric Gershwin and Edwin L. Klingelhofer, in their book *Conquering Your Child's Allergies*, indicate that some allergy medications can increase your child's output of urine and therefore can increase the chances of bedwetting. Among these medications is theophylline, a drug often used to treat asthma. Theophylline is used because it dilates the airways and relieves breathing difficulties, but apparently it also stimulates the kidneys to make more urine.

If your child takes theophylline at bedtime, he will have to urinate at night. If he is a heavy sleeper, he may not awaken, and he may wet his bed. Discuss this problem with the doctor who is treating the asthma and ask for an alternative medication if you think this is your child's problem. See whether a change in medication makes a difference.

5

SECONDARY BEDWETTING

H as your child begun bedwetting after having been dry for about six
months or more? Perhaps for years? If so, you are certainly per-
plexed about what is causing this new wetting and what you can do
about it.

Bedwetting that begins after a long period of dryness is called
secondary bedwetting. It has many different causes. In a small number
of children, it is caused by diseases such as diabetes mellitus or kidney
diseases (discussed in the preceding chapter). In other children, secondary bedwetting is caused by:

- A cold, flu, or other illness.
- An illness in the incubation stage (doesn't show yet).
- Any infection in the body.
- A flare-up of a previous, underlying condition (in children who
  urinate frequently and urgently in the daytime).
- An episode of constipation (chapter 6 will explain how constipation
  can contribute to bedwetting).
- A cold bedroom or insufficient blankets.
- A large intake of liquids, especially those containing caffeine (tea,
  coffee, colas, many other carbonated drinks).
- Pinworms.
- Sleep apnea.
- A change of circumstances in life that seems overwhelmingly threat-
  ening to your child, such as the start of school, the birth of a new
  sister or brother, separation from parents and siblings, or a death or
  divorce in the family.

Sometimes secondary bedwetting is long-term and persistent, and sometimes, of course, it is short-lived or just a brief episode.

FIRST, VISIT THE DOCTOR

First, arrange for your pediatrician or family doctor to examine your child and to rule out such diseases and conditions as a cold or flu, diabetes, pinworms, an infection, inflammation of the anal or genital areas, hemorrhoids, or other physical conditions or diseases.

Be sure to make a list of any symptoms you observe and to bring it with you to the doctor's office. Is your child much thirstier than usual? More tired than usual? Urinating more frequently during the day or night? Having an unaccustomed bout of constipation? Often scratching or rubbing the anal or genital area? Has your child always had daytime symptoms of frequency and urgency, but previously managed to awaken and get to the toilet at night? (Daytime symptoms may point to an underlying condition in the lower urinary tract or to the development of allergic causes of bedwetting.) Let the doctor know. Be sure that the doctor takes a urine sample. The laboratory can look for sugar in the urine (to rule out diabetes), specific gravity of the urine (to tell if the kidney is concentrating urine properly), and bacteria (to rule out infection).

If your doctor finds a medical problem, treatment can begin.

Pinworms

Many parents feel enormously embarrassed when pinworms occur in their children. If pinworms are found in your child, do not be embarrassed. These tiny, white, threadlike worms are not confined to any particular social group, neighborhood, or background. They take up lodging in individuals of all ages and socioeconomic classes—as well as in pets. However, most pinworm infestation is found in children, most often in warm or hot climates. Research studies tell us that a greater percentage of children with pinworms wet the bed than do children without pinworms.

Children pick up the worms' eggs on their hands—from toys, sandboxes, bedding, pets, or other children—and put their unwashed hands in their mouths. Or they eat food containing pinworm eggs that has been handled by unwashed hands.

After entering the mouth and being swallowed, the eggs move along and hatch into larvae. When they reach the large intestine, the larvae become adults, and they mate. The females continue down the intestinal tract; finally, they move out of the child's rectal area, usually at night, and deposit their eggs in the moist, creased areas around the anal opening. This causes the area to become itchy and inflamed.

Children then scratch the itchy area (adding to the inflammation) and get more eggs on their hands. If the unwashed hands, or things that the unwashed hands have touched, go into the mouth, reinfestation takes place.

Any inflammation of the anal area, including the inflammation caused by pinworms, can trigger the reflex to urinate and cause your child to wet the bed, especially if he is a heavy sleeper who cannot awaken. (The role that inflammation plays in bedwetting is explained in chapters 2 and 6.)

In addition to inflaming the anal area, pinworms can also work their way into a girl's vagina and urethra and cause inflammation or infection in these areas. This, too, can cause bedwetting.

How do you know if your child has pinworms? There may be very few outward signs. Children with pinworms do not feel or look ill. The most obvious symptoms are the frequent scratching or rubbing of the anal area, and the inflammation of that area. In addition, eventually you may see some threadlike worms in the child's stool.

If you examine the anal area (with the aid of a flashlight) several hours after your child has gone to sleep, you may see worms in the skin folds around the anal opening. Or if you secure a small piece of Scotch tape to a clean ice cream stick or tongue depressor, and press the tape over the anal opening at night, the worms or their eggs will stick to it. You may not be able to see them, but the doctor or laboratory can examine the tape with a low-power microscope to detect them.

If your child has pinworms, he needs a physician's care. The physician will prescribe a medication, such as pyrantel pamoate, for your child to take by mouth, and an ointment to be applied to the inflamed anal area.

In addition, all the bedding, linens, etc., must be laundered, and the hands of everyone in the household must be washed carefully before eating. If one member of the family has pinworms, the infestation may pass along to the other family members and to the household pet. Each one should be examined, and, if necessary, treated.

Sleep Apnea

If your child suffers from sleep apnea (apnea means "without breath"), she has an obstruction such as enlarged tonsils or adenoids, flabby throat muscles, or even a tongue that falls back and blocks the throat during sleep.

The obstruction blocks the flow of air into the lungs, which causes a child to try to breathe harder. However, during sleep, the tissues of the throat and pharynx relax, and the effort to breathe harder makes these tissues come together. To put it another way, when the child tries to inhale deeply, the walls of the airway collapse (the way a straw collapses when it is blocked by a very thick milkshake that you are trying to drink through the straw).

Then, because the child is not breathing (taking in air, expelling carbon dioxide), poisonous carbon dioxide accumulates in the blood. This causes the nervous system to send furious signals to the child to breathe, which awakens her momentarily. She takes one or more large, snorting breaths and falls back to sleep. The apneic occurrence may repeat itself as many as 10 to 100 or more times a night, each lasting from about 10 seconds each to 2 or 3 minutes.

How does this lead to bedwetting? The muscular effort to breathe against a closed airway increases pressure greatly within the abdomen and on the bladder. This pressure, the poor quality of sleep, the loss of muscle tone, and the large amount of urine that the kidneys excrete when they are trying to rid the blood of the accumulated carbon dioxide, together lead to bedwetting.

We know that children with sleep apnea generally snore at night, breathe through their mouths, seem excessively tired and sleepy during the day, complain of headaches, and sometimes show poor school performance (probably because of the poor quality of sleep). About 10 percent of these children sleepwalk.

We do not know how many bedwetting children suffer sleep apnea. Reports do show that only a small number of apneic children become bedwetters (about 1 to 10 percent). However, the condition is not reported frequently, possibly because physicians overlook it. Bedwetting that results from sleep apnea may occur after a period of dryness (secondary wetting), but it may also occur from birth (primary wetting).

If your child shows the symptoms of sleep apnea, you need to take him to a doctor specializing in ear, nose, and throat problems. Both the apnea and the bedwetting can be alleviated or lessened. In 1991, researcher, Dudley J. Weider and associates reported that correction of airway abnormalities produced a cure or a significant lessening of bedwetting in 76 percent of apnea/bedwetting cases. In many cases, sleep apnea is the result of enlarged tonsils or adenoids. For a number of children, the treatment may be as simple as the removal of the tonsils or adenoids.

NEXT, CHECK THE OTHER
PHYSICAL POSSIBILITIES

If your doctor finds no medical problem, reassure your child that the bedwetting is temporary and that you and your spouse are not angry because of it. Check for other possible causes. Make sure your child's room is not too cool and your child is warmly covered at night. Permit normal amounts of usual fluids, but withhold tea, iced tea, coffee, or carbonated beverages containing caffeine. (Caffeinated beverages are natural diuretics—they increase the amount of urine produced by the kidneys. Other natural diuretics you can withhold during the bout of bedwetting include asparagus and raw pineapple.) Check for very large fluid intake, including large amounts of watermelon in season.

FINALLY, CONSIDER STRESSFUL
EVENTS IN YOUR CHILD'S LIFE

Because I am a urologist and not a child psychiatrist, pediatricians who suspect that a child is experiencing the onset of secondary bedwetting as a result of a stressful or traumatic event in the child's life would probably not refer that child to me. Although I believe, along with many others, that primary bedwetting and much secondary wetting are caused by physical factors, many researchers report that secondary bedwetting has psychological causes in a significant number of cases.

I believe that psychological stresses are more likely to cause bedwetting in children who were late in gaining bladder control than in children who gained control early.

In any case, researchers point to stressful changes in a child's life as causes of secondary wetting.

Richard Dalton, author of a chapter in the *Nelson Textbook of Pediatrics*, says, "The . . . [secondary] type of bedwetting is precipitated by stressful environmental events, such as the move to a new home, marital conflict, birth of a sibling, or death in the family."

Thomas F. Anders and Ellen D. Freeman, writing on enuresis in the *Basic Handbook of Child Psychiatry*, Volume 2, add "the loss of a significant adult" and "separation" to the lists of enuresis-provoking events.

And in addition to the "situational stresses" listed by the others, John Werry is reported by Richard O. Carpenter (in *Principles and Practice of Pediatrics*) to point out that "separation from the mother" and "hospitalization of the young child" are among the most common causes of secondary enuresis.

Many other stressors are reported to bring on bedwetting. In his book *The Psychiatric Disorders of Childhood*, Charles R. Shaw describes an interesting case of a 14-year-old girl who suddenly began bedwetting when her father prevented her from dating a boy she was interested in. The bedwetting occurred every night she slept at home, but not on the occasional nights she slept at the home of a favorite aunt.

Studies also report that disasters such as the nuclear disaster at Three-Mile Island and the bombing of London during World War II caused the onset of bedwetting in children affected by them.

If all of the physical causes mentioned earlier in this chapter have been ruled out, you should explore the possibility that conscious or unconscious fears or other distress about a substantial or threatening change in your child's life may be contributing to the new bedwetting.

If such a factor is causing your child's secondary bedwetting, you will need to encourage discussion, calm fears, and give sincere, generous reassurement. Fears are often difficult for a young child to articulate. Without discussion, your child may not be able to bring those hard-to-express fears to the surface and confront them.

The following sections will address some of these possible causes, starting with factors that cause the shortest episodes of wetting and progressing to those that affect children the most seriously—and will attempt to give you sound strategies for coping with them. Some of the suggestions have come not from academic studies, but from parents; I am including them because you may find them helpful.

At the Start of School

If your child has started wetting just as she has begun kindergarten or one of the early elementary grades, and the doctor has found no physical cause of the bedwetting, have patience. Your child, like many others, may be very apprehensive about the unknown new situation and strange teacher; about mastering new work or "not knowing enough" for the new grade level; or simply about being away from the safety, familiarity, and acceptance of parents and home.

You may want to try giving your child some special privilege or privileges to go along with the milestone of entering either kindergarten or a new grade level in school. For example, permit a slightly later bedtime; a role in shopping for the clothes to be worn to school; or a picnic, party, or excursion to which some of the new classmates can be invited. Let your child be in charge of some new aspect of her life.

Be supportive. Share with your child memories of your own early experiences at school. Encourage discussion about experiences at school, the teacher, the classmates, the "best things" and the "worst things" at school. Fasten a sheet of paper on the refrigerator door, and list two or three "best things" and "worst things" that happened at school each day. Discuss them. You may be able to detect and address a real or imagined problem.

For example, if you learn that one of the "worst things" about school is being bullied on the school bus or in the school yard, you need to talk to the bus driver or teacher on duty and see that the situation changes. On the other hand, if the problem is more imagined than real, talking about it will bring it into perspective for your child. Soon, going to school will become routine and unthreatening, and, as parents report, the bedwetting should cease.

When a New Baby Is Born or Adopted

Your formerly dry child may have started bedwetting just as you brought a new infant into the family. Researchers such as Anthony Kales and Richard Dalton say that the birth of a new baby is one of the stressful events that can cause your child to begin wetting again. Allen H. Handford and associates, writing in the textbook *Child and Adolescent Psychiatry*, and other researchers, support this idea.

Your child may feel deeply threatened by the new arrival—fearful of not being loved or wanted any longer and worried about being replaced.

If your doctor has found no physical cause for the bedwetting, you will have to think of ways to make your child feel very much included in the new scheme of things, as well as very special and loved.

One mother told me the following story: Her four-year-old daughter began bedwetting (after more than a year of dryness) when a second daughter was born. The mother did not say a word about the bedwetting. Instead, she considered ways to help her daughter feel grown up and special. Finally, she decided to make an appointment at the hair salon for her young daughter and made sure, with some fanfare, that the girl was treated "just like the grown-up ladies," receiving first a "grown-up" haircut, and then a short session under a hair dryer between two adult customers. Much ado was made by all, and the daughter, who was proud and pleased about this adult experience, stopped wetting immediately!

There are many ways to make your child feel included, loved, useful, and special when a new baby arrives. You can take turns with your spouse accompanying your child in special activities in which only an older child can participate. Doing so will give her the special attention she needs at this time and will make her happy to be more grown up than an infant. Confer with your spouse, and use your creativity.

You may also wish to discuss with your child her feelings about the new baby. Do not scold her if she expresses rejection or hostility. Instead, reassure her that parents are very rich when it comes to love for their children: They have more than enough love for all of their children. Tell her that she will always be as special to you as the day she was born. And suggest to her that her new little brother or sister will soon be another person who not only loves and cares about her but looks up to her as well.

Remember that in this situation your child's bedwetting is very likely a temporary episode: It will pass. And if you deal with it compassionately, it is likely to pass much sooner.

When a Life Ends

The death of a close relative or friend is one of the traumatic events in a child's life that researchers say may cause a dry child to begin bedwetting. In addition to the researchers mentioned earlier in this chapter, others support this idea. In the *Comprehensive Textbook of Psychiatry*, Edwin J. Mikkelsen reports that it is particularly common for boys to develop secondary enuresis following the loss of their father through death or divorce.

Another researcher, Stephen J. Dollinger, investigated the emotional effects on 38 fifth- and sixth-grade children who witnessed a bolt of lightning strike and kill one of their friends at a soccer game. He reported in the *British Journal of Medical Psychology* that some of the children developed anxiety, sleep disturbances, separation anxiety, and bedwetting.

Young children do not fully understand "death," but even the youngest understand more than most adults realize. They know when they see a dead bird or fish or animal that the creature is no longer living, and they feel shocked by that.

When a relative, especially a close relative, dies, children's feelings are complicated by many troubling, often unspoken, misconceptions—and occasionally by the transparent dishonesty of adults who hope to protect the child from the disturbing truth. Some children think that past bad behavior or bad thoughts on their part contributed to the death. Some are afraid to cry or grieve or have been discouraged from doing so. As the researchers have shown, some children begin wetting their beds.

If your child started wetting the bed soon after the death of a relative, encourage discussion of feelings about the death and the relative. Be honest: Don't say that the relative is "sleeping" or that he "went away" or "moved away." The child knows from everyone's sadness and tension, and from everything going on around him, that something terrible has happened. Let your child know that the relative died because of a very bad disease, or very old age, or a bad accident.

The most important things your child needs to hear are that you are not also about to die (and will be around for a long time), that he is not about to die (and has a whole lifetime ahead), and that nothing that he did contributed to the illness or death of the deceased. The loss of a close relative is a life-threatening change that can become terrifying to your child if he fears that the next illness may kill you, another beloved family member, or himself. It can also become a guilt-ridden, personal hell if he imagines that some of his misbehavior, anger, or "bad" thoughts helped to cause the death.

It's important to let your child know that crying and sadness are perfectly normal, to encourage questions, and to answer those questions honestly, to the best of your ability.

Your child's bedwetting will not continue forever. However, you will most likely bring it to a much speedier conclusion if you act on the suggestions in this section.

When Parents Divorce

The researchers referred to earlier in this chapter agree that divorce and separation of parents can cause a child who has been dry to begin secondary bedwetting. In addition, a group of researchers led by Irma Moilanen, at the University of Oulu, Finland, studied 156 enuretic and 170 nonenuretic seven-year-old children and reported that nonenuretic children more commonly lived with their original families and with both biological parents, while enuretic children had more commonly experienced parental divorce or separation. And Marjo R. Jarvelin and associates, of the same university, studying 30 different life events in the same children, found that the single life change most apt to cause secondary wetting was the divorce or separation of the parents (or separation from one of the parents for some other reason).

It is not surprising that even more threatening to a child than a death in the family is the divorce of one's parents. Generally, the child understands that a person who dies does not do so by choice; but when parents separate or divorce, at least one of them chooses to do so. Although children in this situation may not verbalize it, they often feel that they are about to be abandoned and that the world is ending. Many suffer secret guilt, believing that in some way they helped to cause the divorce, and fearing that their parents hate them.

If your child's bedwetting started with your separation or divorce, and your physician could find no physical cause, it may last much longer than wetting caused by some other life stressors.

You and your ex-spouse must reassure all of your children that you are separating for reasons of your own that are very important to you but that have nothing to do with anything that your children have or haven't done; that you both love your children very much and will always love them; and that even if you have different living arrangements, you will always, always be their parents.

Give your children permission to cry and grieve, and plenty of opportunity to ventilate feelings, including fear and anger. Let them know that you truly understand how they feel. Also give them as many positive ideas about the future as possible. Let them be a part of the planning for some future aspects of their lives, such as the rearrangement of their bedroom furniture, layout of a new garden, and division of chores in the family. Do not single out the bedwetting child for different treatment from the other children.

Additional measures will help to rebuild your child's sense of security and well-being. Both you and your ex-spouse need to make generous amounts of time available to be with the children. And difficult as it may be, you must both avoid saying negative things about each other to the children. Unless one of the parents has been abusing the children, they absolutely need to love and respect both parents.

In addition, both parents must avoid trying to outdo each other in an attempt to be the favorite parent. At some level the child understands that one parent's unusual permissiveness, excessive gifts, or other campaign to curry favor has more to do with competing with the divorced spouse than about love for the child. Above all, do your best to provide a healthy, structured environment in which your child has duties, responsibilities, privileges, a sense of belonging, and love. As all of the family members adjust to the new situation and settle down to a constructive routine of life, the bedwetter will eventually stop wetting.

If the situation becomes too difficult to handle alone, consider arranging for your children to visit a child psychologist, child psychiatrist, family counselor, or minister. If you think you can't afford private assistance, look for family service organizations in your area that offer reduced-cost or even no-cost counseling. Your minister, priest, or rabbi, your local school's guidance counselor, or the social worker employed in a nearby hospital will be able to inform you of the nearest social service or family service agencies. A telephone call to any of these people will be sufficient. You may also find the agency you need in the yellow pages or blue pages of the local telephone book.

When the Child Is Separated from the Family

Researchers Z. A. Stein and M. W. Susser studied the effects of separation on children, and they reported in *Developmental Medicine and Child Neurology* that a higher incidence of bedwetting is caused by placement of children in the care of others when their own families cannot take care of them than is caused by other types of life stressors.

Anthony L. Pillay and his associates conducted a study on secondary bedwetting in institutionalized children and reported in *Psychological Reports* that 62 percent of these children had become bedwetters within six months of being removed from home. (Earlier researchers K. S. Dittman and K. A. Blinn reported that up to 30 percent of institutionalized children bedwet.) Pillay's group concluded that removing children from their families needs to be reexamined and that "prolonged or complete separation from the family should be avoided wherever possible."

It is true that a desperately difficult situation can arise in life that may force parents to place children with grandparents, other relatives, boarding schools, children's shelters, or even in correctional institutions. Still, the impact of the separation on the child is extremely traumatic. Even children with loving parents experience intense anxiety: They fear that their parents are rejecting them and that they are to be separated from their families forever. They experience guilt, believing that something they did contributed to the separation.

If the new caregiver reports that your child has started bedwetting, you should not skip the first step, even though you may be far away: Arrange for someone to take your child to a doctor near the new location. If the doctor can find no physical cause of the new bedwetting, take as many constructive steps as possible.

Encourage discussion on the telephone and in visits. Let your child know that you are aware of how distressful the separation must be for him and that it is okay to cry and to be fearful and angry. Don't belittle your child's fears; try to understand them. Let your child know that the separation is hurting you, too. If the separation was not caused by the child's delinquent behavior, assure him that he did not contribute to it and was not responsible for it. Reassure him of your love as often as possible.

Find out whether some condition at the temporary location is particularly upsetting to your child, and see if any appropriate changes can be made. Also, encourage him to discuss all the interesting things at the temporary home, so he can begin to see some positive aspects of the new situation.

Supply plenty of self-addressed, stamped envelopes, paper, and postcards so your child can write to you easily (or can dictate messages to an adult writer). Let your child know that these messages mean a great deal to you. Write to your child every day—even if just a postcard. Call as often as possible.

If the doctor is correct in finding that nothing is medically wrong with your child, the bedwetting should eventually stop, although it may take longer than you may wish.

Of course, if the separation has been caused by the institutionalization of your child because of seriously delinquent behavior, it will be important for you and other family members to receive counseling and for your child to receive long-term professional help.

WHAT TO REMEMBER IN ALL OF THESE SITUATIONS

Remember that your child is not bedwetting deliberately (she truly can't help it). Certain kinds of physical conditions and psychological situations simply have this effect on the urinary system in some children.

You probably understand that bedwetting caused by a physical effect on the urinary system is beyond your child's control. But the same is true of secondary bedwetting caused by deep fear and anxiety. Think of situations in which anxiety affected your urinary system: the time you almost wet your pants on the way to the principal's office, even though you had done nothing wrong; the time you did wet your pants when a bully came after you; or the time you had to go to the bathroom in the middle of an important final exam at school, despite having been to the bathroom twice before you entered the exam room. Think about the time you learned you were in danger of losing your job, and how you found yourself running to the bathroom every half hour. Were you able to control these effects?

Now think of a child who is burdened with life-shaking fears. Does it seem so strange that she could experience a return of bedwetting? The most important thing to avoid is any temptation to berate or ridicule or punish this child. Don't be angry; don't be "disappointed"; don't be "sad." Be compassionate. Be constructive. Most of all, be patient.

If your child's bedwetting seems to be continuing more than a week or two and the doctor can find no physical cause, be sure to let your child know that it has a cause. Discuss with him the probability that the bedwetting and his feelings about some problem are connected and that talking about the problem will help him to feel better and to stop wetting his bed. Let him know that you will listen to his concerns and that you care about them.

Remember, do not jump to the conclusion that the wetting is caused by psychological factors. Investigate physical causes first and if the wetting persists for more than a few weeks or months, you may want to take your child to another doctor. The first one may have overlooked an important physical cause.

6

CONSTIPATION, ENCOPRESIS, HEMORRHOIDS, OR INFLAMMATIONS CAN BE CULPRITS

Does your bedwetting child have problems with constipation or with another bowel condition called "encopresis" (an involuntary passage of stool)? Have you detected external hemorrhoids at the anal opening? Are your child's anal or genital areas inflamed?

These problems can cause daytime urinary symptoms (frequent, urgent urination) and, if your child is a heavy sleeper, can also cause bedwetting. (If you have not read chapter 2, which discusses the anatomy, please go back and read it. It will help you understand how the physical problems discussed here contribute to bedwetting.)

According to researchers Sean O'Regan and Salam Yazbeck, who reported their findings in the journal *Medical Hypotheses*, frequent constipation (solid waste that is too hard and difficult to pass from the body) is the cause of bedwetting in about 15 percent of bedwetters. These researchers also found that correction of the constipation relieves bedwetting in 67 percent of the children who have both problems.

Small anal hemorrhoids and painful splits in the anal lining (fissures), which are generally caused by passage of hard, dry stools, are related causes of bedwetting.

Also, the condition called *encopresis*—involuntary passage of stool,

73

especially overly soft stool, into the underclothing—can cause bedwetting.

Finally, constipation, encopresis, hemorrhoids, fissures, and other conditions can cause irritation and inflammation. Irritation or inflammation of the anal area and canal in children of both sexes, along with infection or inflammation of the genital area in girls, cause more bedwetting than many physicians and parents suspect. If your child's pediatrician or family doctor fails to inspect your child's genital and anal areas carefully to look for inflammation, external hemorrhoids, or other abnormalities, you ought to request tactfully that this be done.

How can such conditions cause or contribute to bedwetting and daytime urinary problems?

HOW CONSTIPATION, ENCOPRESIS, AND INFLAMMATIONS CAUSE BEDWETTING

As you remember from chapter 2, both the urinary and anal canals contain branches from the same nerves and blood vessels. Therefore, things that affect one area affect the other.

Constipation, Hemorrhoids, Fissures, and Inflammations

With constipation, your child's rectum is full of stool that crowds the bladder and reduces the capacity of the bladder. This causes a need to urinate more frequently, both in the daytime and at night. If your child is a heavy sleeper, she may not awaken to urinate and may wet the bed.

In addition, if your child's rectum is crowding the bladder, it is creating pressures that interfere with the draining of blood from the blood vessels of both the urethral and anal canals. If the interference is frequent, it can cause dilated or swollen veins (hemorrhoids). Hemorrhoids, as well as inflammations of the anal areas and painful fissures that are caused by passage of hard stools, throw the sphincter muscles into spasms. When the urethral sphincter muscles tighten, they interfere with the free flow of urine. Because of this blockage, the urine flow exerts high pressures on the walls of the urethra, which in turn causes inflammation of the urethral walls, sensitive nerve endings in the urethra, and a weakening of the urethral muscles (sphincters). The sequence of abnormal pressures, overly sensitive nerve endings, and weakened sphincters triggers uncontrollable, involuntary urination during sleep and, in some children, even in the daytime.

Encopresis (Involuntary Passage of Stool)

According to Jane E. Brody, health writer for *The New York Times*, 1 percent to 2 percent of children over age four suffer from involuntary soiling with stool, and the problem is much more common in boys than in girls.

As many physicians note, if your child suffers from encopresis, he involuntarily passes some stool—often loose, watery stool—into underclothing, where it remains in contact with the skin for a time. Melvin D. Levine, chief of ambulatory pediatrics at Boston's Children's Hospital, noted in a review of the subject in *Pediatrics in Review* that at different times "the same child may stain, soil, emit little 'rocks,' and pass whole movements." The stool carries many bacteria. Whether it is just a stain or a larger movement, the stool inflames the skin it touches.

In addition, after passing very loose bowel movements in the toilet, your child may not be able to sufficiently cleanse away the residue of stool adhering to the skin around the anus. (More than toilet paper alone is necessary for loose stools: A gentle follow-up with paper towels wet with lukewarm water is the minimum requirement.)

Any inflammation of your child's anal, genital, or urinary area increases pressure on the nerve endings in those areas, including the nerve endings involved in the urinating reflexes. Pressure on these nerve endings causes them to discharge too soon. Once the urinating reflexes are triggered, especially in sleep, they are beyond your child's control. (See chapter 2 for a detailed explanation of how the urinary reflexes are triggered.)

DETECTING BOWEL PROBLEMS AND HEMORRHOIDS

If your child has a bowel problem, especially constipation, it is possible that you are not aware of it. As is the case with many parents who do not wish to become unhealthily preoccupied with their children's bowel movement routines, you may have simply not noticed. Or your child's urinary problem may have drawn your attention away from it.

Does Your Child Have Constipation or Encopresis?

How do you know when your child has a bowel problem? You need to be able to answer these questions:

- Does your child have a bowel movement each day, or does he frequently skip one or more days?
- Does the bowel movement come easily, or does your child strain to move his bowels?
- Is there pain with a bowel movement?
- Does your child complain of "tummy aches"?
- Does your child stain or soil his underpants with stool?

You should suspect a bowel problem if your child does not have a bowel movement each day, strains to pass his stool, complains of belly aches, or soils his underpants with stool. (If your child's underpants are stained with stool, this staining is probably not the result of hasty wiping or improper hygiene, as many people think, but the result of abnormal stool consistency or abnormal anal canal function.)

Some children suffer alternately with constipation and encopresis; their stools are too solid and difficult to pass for a time, and then loose, watery stools make their way around the blockage and pass involuntarily. This alternating pattern is true of most (although not all) children who experience encopresis.

In questioning your child about bowel problems, be sure to explain that you need this important information for the doctor. Make your child a partner in the detecting process.

Does Your Child Empty Her
Bowels Incompletely?

Sometimes children move their bowels daily, but only partially empty the rectum, a condition that can also cause bedwetting. If you wish to check for partial emptying yourself, you can wait until just after your child completes a bowel movement and then insert a pediatric (child-size) glycerine suppository into her rectum. If the suppository causes her to produce more feces at this time, then emptying has been incomplete. Before performing this procedure, of course, be sure to explain gently to your child what the procedure will tell you and why it is necessary to know this.

If you find that your child's bowels are not emptying completely, you should tell this to the doctor.

If you do not feel comfortable about subjecting your child to a suppository, you can ask the doctor to conduct an examination by ultrasound. This method is not invasive, and it would be less stressful for both you and your child.

Does Your Child Have Hemorrhoids?

If the stool remains too long in your child's rectum it hardens, and when your child finally passes such a stool, it can cause anal canal irritation or a painful split (fissure) in the delicate anal lining. Fearing pain, your child may delay passing stool. The cycle is repeated again and again: hard stools, anal irritation or fissure, and delayed movement. Hemorrhoids, a result of this cycle and of straining to pass the hardened or overly large stool, occur more frequently among children than most physicians suspect.

Hemorrhoids can occur externally (at the anal opening) or internally (inside the anus). You yourself can easily see any external hemorrhoids, which are bluish, raised areas at the opening of the anal canal. (Be sure to explain gently to your child what you are looking for—and why it is important to know this information.)

You will not be able to detect internal hemorrhoids; even the physician cannot detect them in an ordinary physical exam.

THE CAUSES OF CONSTIPATION
AND ENCOPRESIS

The causes of constipation and encopresis are not completely understood, but they are not the result of an emotional disorder or improper toilet training, as some parents (and even some physicians) think. According to Jane Brody, Dr. Edward R. Christophersen of Children's Mercy Hospital in Kansas City, Missouri, believes that most cases of encopresis result from chronic constipation:

> Eventually, colon tissues stretch to the point that nerves fail to receive proper signals and the muscles can no longer contract properly to expel wastes. Eventually, stool pushes its way around impacted fecal matter, and soiling results. Because of nerve and muscle stretching, children with the problem typically say they didn't feel it coming, and they may not even be aware of an accident after it has occurred.

Brody also reports:

> The child may have been born with poor muscle tone in the bowel or a poorly functioning anal sphincter. Bowel control can be complicated by underlying medical problems like painful anal fissures or chronic diarrhea caused by food intolerances, gastroenteritis [inflammation of the stomach and intestine], or ulcerative colitis.

Many writers note that intolerances to certain foods such as milk, cheese, and other milk products cause bowel problems in some children. A diet that lacks the necessary amount of fiber and fluid can also cause these problems. Occasionally there are anatomic problems, such as a narrowing of the anus, or underlying diseases such as smooth muscle disease or endocrine abnormalities. Also, very rarely, there may be metabolic or neurological causes. In addition, there is a rare disease called "Hirschsprung's disease" (or "aganglionic megacolon"), which causes severe constipation. (Children with this disease have it from birth.) To rule out any of these rare causes of bowel problems, your child should be examined by a doctor.

TREATING BOWEL PROBLEMS, HEMORRHOIDS, AND INFLAMMATIONS

If your bedwetting child suffers from constipation, encopresis, hemorrhoids, or inflammations of the anal or genital areas, successful treatment of that condition is likely to cure or significantly reduce the bedwetting and daytime urinary symptoms. Treatment may require patience and attempts at more than one treatment plan over time, but the results can be very rewarding.

Treating Constipation and Encopresis

The treatments for constipation and encopresis are very similar. First, your child needs to be examined by a physician who can rule out or treat possible diseases or anatomical conditions.

Then you can investigate dietary changes. Normal bowel movement and control require both adequate stool bulk and an adequate amount of moisture in the stool. Your child may simply need more insoluble fiber in the diet. One excellent source of insoluble fiber is unprocessed wheat bran ("miller's bran"), which you can find on the cereal shelf at the supermarket or in health food stores; it often works wonders.

You can mix the bran thoroughly with a very moist food, or you can cook with bran. Alternate by mixing the bran with tuna salad, soup, meat loaf, scrambled eggs, applesauce, or baked goods. The effective amount of bran varies from one individual to the next, so you must use trial and error to determine the best amount. Start with a teaspoonful to a tablespoonful per day, depending on the age and size of the child. You do not want to overdo it; too much bran can produce irritation and other gastrointestinal symptoms. Also, be careful never to give dry bran by itself to your child; dry bran causes choking. Always mix the bran with very moist or wet food.

Serve whole grains: whole wheat bread instead of white bread, unpolished brown rice instead of polished white rice. Be sure your child eats several fiber-rich salad vegetables, cooked vegetables, and raw fruits every day. Baked beans, potatoes, and berries are excellent sources of fiber. In addition, be sure your child drinks a sufficient amount of fluids (especially with the meals that contain extra bran).

Because some foods—such as chocolate, dairy products, and wheat products—may be particularly binding in some children and produce the opposite extreme in others, you may want to keep your child from eating them for a while to see if their absence makes a difference. However, be sure to supplement with calcium if you withhold milk and cheese. A form of calcium supplement that also contains magnesium is especially useful in constipation because, while supplying the necessary calcium and magnesium that the body needs, the magnesium also relieves constipation. You can ask for a calcium/magnesium supplement in your pharmacy or health food store (no prescription is required).

You may want to try withholding other foods that you suspect may be causing your child to have bowel problems. (Two or three weeks of withholding the suspected food should be a sufficient trial period.) Since bowel problems may be caused by intolerances to certain foods, you may want to follow the steps of an elimination diet described in the chapter on food intolerances. (See chapter 7.)

Like all of us, children need activity and exercise to maintain regularity. Don't let your child become a "couch potato." School-age children especially need exercise because they sit at desks most of the school day and then come home to sit and do homework and to watch television in the evening. If this is true of your child, try to put more physical activity in his schedule.

In "the old days" parents administered laxatives and/or enemas to their constipated children. According to several researchers, you should not administer either one to your child unless your doctor has instructed you to do so. They may cause considerable physical pain and distress. They also cause psychological distress in young children who misinterpret the purpose. Among other things, the frightened children believe that their parents are meting out punishment, not attempting to cure them.

Do not punish your child for soiling. Remember that your child can't help it.

Above all, it is very important that you call any continuing bowel symptoms, however slight, to the attention of your child's pediatrician, who will have additional methods of treating constipation and/or encopresis.

In difficult cases of constipation, your doctor may prescribe stool softeners or try other measures.

When the bowel problems are relieved, the bedwetting will very likely be relieved as well.

Treating Hemorrhoids

Your child's physician can detect external hemorrhoids (those on the outside of the anus) very easily. Unfortunately, internal hemorrhoids are not detectable by a physician's external examination, nor by examination with a gloved finger.

Hemorrhoids in children are caused by constipation and are reversible. They do not require surgery. If your child has hemorrhoids, treatment of the constipation that causes them will very likely cure them. In the meanwhile, remind your child to avoid straining to pass stool. Straining contributes to the development of hemorrhoids.

Ask your child's doctor about additional methods of treating the hemorrhoids.

Treating Irritation and Inflammation

If your child has any redness or soreness on or around the anal or genital area, bring this condition to the attention of your child's doctor, who will investigate the cause. Irritation and inflammation of the anal or genital area can be caused by many different things, such as leakage of stool, an infection, or pinworms. The treatment will depend on the cause.

During the investigation and possible treatment of any of the problems addressed in this chapter, remember that these underlying causes of bedwetting are not your child's fault—just as the bedwetting is not your child's fault. Explain as much as you can at your child's level of comprehension, bolster your child's sense of self-respect, and be very understanding of the stresses that poking, prodding, examining, and questioning surely cause your child to experience.

7

CONSIDER ALLERGIES AND FOOD INTOLERANCES

From what you have read in this book so far, you know that bedwetting has a number of different causes. The challenge is to identify the one responsible for *your* child's bedwetting. If your child's pediatrician has ruled out the possibilities discussed in the preceding chapters, your next step is to find out whether an allergy or intolerance to some substance or substances may be to blame. Can reactions to substances cause bedwetting? This issue is controversial. Some physicians say "no," while others say "yes, in a small number of cases."

As a urologist, I have not treated children's allergies and food intolerances, and I have no experience with allergic bedwetting. However, I have read the professional literature on the relationship of these problems to bedwetting, and I am aware of some anecdotal evidence as well. I'll attempt to acquaint you with some researchers' findings on how allergies and intolerances may contribute to your child's bedwetting. I'll also discuss the methods of diagnosing these problems, and the ways of treating them. Clearly, more research needs to be done in this area. But in the meantime, it may be worth investigating before you agree to surgery to correct your child's bedwetting.

We know that an allergy or intolerance to certain foods, chemicals, molds, animal hair, feathers, house dust mites, or other substances may cause one or more of the following conditions:

- Hay fever
- Asthma
- Eczema
- Abdominal pain
- Nasal congestion

- Fatigue
- Leg aches
- Hives, skin rashes
- Headaches
- Canker sores (mouth sores)
- Inflammation of the urethra and/or bladder
- Hyperactivity/attention deficit disorder

Allergies to the same kinds of substances might also cause long-term bedwetting, as well as daytime urinary frequency and urgency, in some children.

ALLERGIES OR INTOLERANCES?

There are important scientific differences between true allergies and intolerances. There are also some important practical similarities. (Although applied to children throughout this discussion, these concepts apply to adults as well.)

Allergies

In a true allergy, a substance that your body doesn't like (an allergen) enters your body, and your body responds by producing a special antibody called *immunoglobulin E* (or *IgE*). This antibody is produced to counteract the allergen, and it has a special affinity for the cell membranes of special cells called *mast cells*, which are found in tissues throughout the body. It attaches itself to the outsides of mast cells and in this way remains fixed in various tissues.

Later, when the same allergen—such as shellfish or walnut, for example—makes another contact in your body, an antigen-antibody reaction occurs. This causes the mast cells in the tissue to break down and release *histamine*, which in turn causes inflammation of the area, or, in extreme cases, anaphylactic shock. (Anaphylactic shock is an extreme allergic reaction that can cause swelling in the lungs, heart failure, and even death. You may have heard of penicillin or bee stings causing people who are allergic to them to go into this state of shock.)

Allergens cause some reactions to start within a very short time (sometimes only minutes) and some within a longer period (hours) after contact. And while this is, as I said, still controversial, some researchers believe that allergens can cause a variety of physical and behavioral symptoms—including bedwetting.

According to the *1992 Report of the Royal College of Physicians Committee on Immunology and Allergy* (British) and to many researchers, allergies run in families; they are inherited.

True allergies can be relieved by *antihistamines* (such as Benadryl) and by allergy shots. Of course, they can also be relieved by completely avoiding the substance or substances that cause the reaction.

Researchers generally recognize that true allergies can often be detected by skin prick ("scratch") tests and radio-allergo-absorbent tests (RASTs), although these tests are not completely accurate or foolproof.

Researchers Eugene P. McCarty and Oscar L. Frick reported in the *Journal of Pediatrics* that the foods that most commonly cause true, histamine-releasing allergies are cow's milk, peanuts, eggs, soy foods, seafood, and nuts. Most allergy researchers agree on this, and add corn to the list.

Intolerances

Intolerances are a bit trickier than allergies. According to certain researchers, such as William G. Crook, many foods and other substances can cause physical and behavioral problems, including bedwetting, in your child without causing his body to produce IgE or release histamine. Instead, these substances are thought to have some other allergylike or disturbing effect on the body. The body is *intolerant* to them rather than allergic to them.

Researchers also report that the effects of intolerances may take longer to be seen than allergies (sometimes several days), and the effects may last longer. They cannot be relieved by antihistamines. Laboratory tests do not detect these offending substances, although some researchers use a method of placing a suspected substance under the tongue and watching for reactions. (This method, which is quite controversial and distrusted by many physicians, is called *sublingual testing*.) According to most researchers, the only way you can truly identify a food intolerance is with the use of some form of *elimination diet*, which I'll describe later in this chapter.

Researchers McCarty and Frick (mentioned above), along with most authorities, agree that cow's milk and gluten are the substances that most frequently cause intolerances (including celiac disease). Gluten, a mixture of two proteins, is found in wheat and rye. Many researchers have found intolerances caused by various other substances as well.

Similarities Between Allergies and Intolerances

A true allergen is not harmful to all people. A substance that creates allergies in one person is perfectly harmless in another. In fact, most of us are not affected by that substance at all. No doubt you've met people who are allergic to shellfish, aspirin, or dust, for example—substances that do not bother the majority of people.

The same is true for intolerances. A substance that causes an intolerance in one person is tolerated perfectly well in another. The foods and substances that some say cause a variety of mysterious behavioral and physical problems (including bedwetting and daytime urinary frequency and urgency) in some children have no ill effects at all in most children.

On a practical level, it is very difficult to tell the difference between allergies and intolerances. According to many published papers, both conditions seem to cause similar problems, and the best treatments for both are simply to eliminate the offending substances. So you may find that some people group allergies and intolerances together and call them all by the same name. Some call them "allergies"; some call them "intolerances"; some call them "sensitivities."

CAN ALLERGIES AND INTOLERANCES REALLY CAUSE BEDWETTING?

Because of the articles in medical journals and the anecdotal evidence on the subject, you should consider the possibility that allergies and intolerances cause bedwetting in a small percentage of children. In this section I'll give you the highlights of some research that finds this link. (If you are not interested in the research, skip to the next section, "Symptoms of Allergies and Intolerances.")

One of the earliest physicians to find a connection between offending substances and bedwetting was George W. Bray, who published several articles on it in the early 1930s in the British journals *Archives of Diseases in Childhood* and *British Journal of Children's Diseases* and in his book *Recent Advances in Allergy*. In the course of eliminating allergens to relieve conditions (such as hay fever and asthma) in many patients, he discovered that about 5 percent of his patients had also been bedwetters and had been cured of their bedwetting while being treated for allergies. He reported that these children obtained relief from their bedwetting through antiallergic treatment or by avoiding certain foods. In a few children, the substances responsible for the bedwetting were different from the ones causing the other allergic symptoms, but in many of these children the same substances were responsible for both.

According to Bray, discovering the substances that caused the allergic conditions and keeping those substances out of the child's diet and environment cured or significantly lessened the child's bedwetting and other allergic problems.

Although Bray's results have not been replicated, he deserves credit for his pioneering work in this field.

In 1959 a Hungarian researcher, I. Pastinszky, reported in *Urologia Internationalis* that the same allergic reaction that can cause inflammation and bronchial spasms in the respiratory system can also cause inflammation and spasms in the bladder. Thus the allergies that cause the lungs to become obstructed can also cause the bladder to contract and empty.

In 1969 M. Esperance and John W. Gerard, of the University of Saskatchewan Department of Pediatrics, published an article in the *Canadian Medical Association Journal* comparing the effects of an elimination diet and a drug (imipramine) on bedwetting in 50 children. These children were not chosen because of any accompanying allergies but simply because of their history of bedwetting.

Of the 50 children, 24 were initially placed on a restricted diet that contained no milk, milk products, eggs, citrus fruits, citrus juices, tomatoes, tomato products, chocolate, cocoa, or beverages with artificial coloring.

The authors reported that elimination of these substances stopped the bedwetting in 4 of the 24 children (approximately 17 percent of this group). Bedwetting lessened in an additional few children. (In the remaining children there was either little or no improvement.) It is interesting that in the other group of 26 children who were placed initially on imipramine, 2 of the children whose bedwetting did not stop with imipramine did respond later to the special diet. This research, although very limited, suggests that food allergies and intolerances are linked to bedwetting in at least some children.

In 1975 the allergist William G. Crook published an article in the journal *Pediatric Clinics of North America* on the role of food allergies and intolerances in a syndrome he called the "allergic tension-fatigue syndrome." He listed many symptoms, including tiredness, depression, irritability, pallor, dark circles under the eyes, stuffy or runny nose, recurrent ear infections, headaches, leg aches, and unusual sensitivity to light, noise, and pain. And he also listed a number of associated symptoms, including bedwetting.

Crook held that foods to which a child is allergic or intolerant can cause spasms of the smooth muscles of the bladder, leading to urinary frequency, decreased ability to hold urine during the day, and bedwetting at night.

In this article and later ones, the offending substances that Crook mentioned most in relation to the "tension-fatigue syndrome" were milk, corn products, wheat products, cane sugar, eggs, chocolate, citrus fruits, food colors and additives, and pollen. He also suspected any substances that the child craved more than others (food addictions) as well as substances that the child disliked.

Crook assumed that eliminating the offending substances would relieve the allergic tension-fatigue syndrome, along with accompanying symptoms such as bedwetting, daytime frequency, and urgency.

In 1982 researchers John F. Simonds and Humberto Parraga reported in the *Hillside Journal of Clinical Psychiatry* that their study of 309 children showed that significantly more children who had ear, nose, and throat allergies wet their beds than did children without allergies.

In 1985 I. Jakobsson, a researcher in Sweden, reported in the journal *Klinishe Padiatrie* an interesting case study of a boy with eczema, bronchial asthma, severe constipation, speech difficulties, and bedwetting. The boy was a heavy milk drinker. When milk was eliminated from his diet, most symptoms disappeared, including the bedwetting and speech difficulties. Later, his parents tried reintroducing milk several times, and each time, the symptoms returned. When the boy was 10 years old, a double-blind "challenge" was performed, meaning he was given some foods with disguised milk and some foods with no milk, while neither he nor his doctors knew which was which. Only the foods with milk caused a return of the bedwetting and speech problems.

In 1992 researchers J. Egger and colleagues, at the Hospital for Sick Children and Institute of Child Health in London, England, reported in the journal *Clinical Pediatrics* on their study of 21 children aged $3^1/2$ to 14 years, who suffered with bedwetting as well as with either migraine headaches or hyperactivity. Some of these children were enuretic during the daytime as well as during the night.

The children were put on a very restricted diet of foods that generally do not cause allergies or intolerances. Those children who did not improve on the first diet were then put on a different, very restricted diet consisting of a different group of foods. The researchers reported that wetting stopped in 12 children and lessened in an additional 4 children. The other symptom (migraine or hyperactivity) stopped in these children as well.

One by one, various additional foods were reintroduced into the diets of the 16 children whose bedwetting and other symptoms had stopped or significantly improved. Some of these foods caused the problems to recur and were removed from that child's diet. Chief among the offending foods were chocolate, milk, and citrus fruits, but at least 19 other foods caused recurrences in one or more children. One child's bedwetting recurred on one food only, but most relapsed on several. One relapsed on eight different foods.

When an offending food was reintroduced, it took one to seven days for it to provoke bedwetting again (most often the time interval was two to three days). Recovery from bedwetting after the offending food was withheld took the same length of time.

All of these findings mean that we cannot ignore the possibility that allergies and intolerances can cause bedwetting, even if the number of children affected by this is small.

SYMPTOMS OF ALLERGIES AND INTOLERANCES

Many researchers point to symptoms you can look for in trying to decide whether your child is allergic or intolerant to any substances. In his book *Helping Your Hyperactive Child*, medical writer John F. Taylor echoes the words of many researchers when he suggests that parents look at these symptoms. Go through this list from his book to see if you notice any of them in your child:

- *Facial symptoms:* glassy or glazed eyes, dark circles under eyes, wrinkles or puffiness below eyes, itchy or watery eyes, swollen eyelids, swollen or cracked lips, reddened earlobes, facial paleness, red cheek patches, itchy nose.
- *Head symptoms:* nasal stuffiness, sniffling, clucking sounds, frequent throat clearing, coughing, wheezing, frequent ear infections, frequent headaches, sudden ear pain, profound ringing in ears, excessive thirst, bad breath.
- *Digestive symptoms:* nausea, bloating, passing of gas, diarrhea, constipation.
- *Skin and muscle symptoms:* itchy rashes (especially in arm or leg creases), frequent muscle and leg aches.
- *... [Other] symptoms:* irritability, belligerence, depression, silly behavior, tantrums, sleep disturbances, bedwetting, sudden mental confusion and absentmindedness, daytime bowel and bladder control problems, overactivity.

Other researchers also include hay fever; asthma; eczema; abdominal pain; fatigue; sluggishness; sleepiness; unusual sensitivity to noise, light, or pain; and a sense of unreality. The researchers say that a child will certainly not have all of these symptoms, or even most of them, but will most likely have a few of them on a regular basis if allergies or intolerances are present. Keep in mind that some researchers believe that bedwetting may be the *only* symptom of food allergy or intolerance in a very few children.

ELIMINATING SUSPECTED FOODS, CHEMICALS, AND INHALANTS

If you think that your bedwetting child may have some of the symptoms listed above or if you want to explore the possibility that her bedwetting is the single symptom of an allergy or intolerance, you may want to try eliminating suspected substances from contact with your child.

Eliminate Milk and Milk Products First

The substance that researchers mention most frequently in connection with bedwetting is *cow's milk,* so I recommend you first try to eliminate

- Wheat and wheat products, including bread, cake, cookies, pasta, noodles, and wheat cereals.
- Vegetables in the nightshade family: tomatoes (also tomato sauces, pasta sauces, tomato juice), potatoes, eggplants, and peppers of all types.
- Citrus fruits, especially oranges. (Some researchers report that grapefruits can be tolerated when oranges cannot.)
- Pork (as well as bacon, ham, lard, and other pork products).
- Chocolate: chocolate candy, hot cocoa, chocolate milk, chocolate cake, icing, cookies, etc.
- One or more types of nuts. (Walnuts and peanuts are mentioned most frequently.)
- Colas, tea, coffee, and other caffeinated beverages.
- Condiments such as catsup and mustard.
- Aspirin and other sources of salicylates.
- Other possibilities: any food or drink that your child particularly craves and any food or drink that your child genuinely dislikes.

Your allergist may recommend eliminating all of these foods from your child's diet for about four weeks. During this period try to give your child the foods that reportedly cause the fewest reactions, such as rice and rice products, lamb, turkey (not self-basted), pears, and many other fruits and vegetables that are not on the list above. Be sure to give your child vitamin supplements.

To plan a diet well balanced for proteins, carbohydrates, fats, vitamins, fiber, and fluids within the limitations and restrictions of the elimination diet, I recommend that you ask your physician for the name of a reputable dietitian or nutritionist who can assist you. Be sure to acquaint this professional thoroughly with your child's special needs.

The elimination diet will work best if you keep a food and bedwetting diary for your child. The diary will help you sort out which foods cause your child to wet and which do not. Keep a page for each day, and at each meal list the foods eaten. Keep track of snacks, too. At the bottom of the page indicate whether the bed was wet or dry that night. Also note any other allergic symptoms you observe.

If bedwetting stops or lessens significantly, you will probably be asked to reintroduce the withheld foods, one food per week, by giving a good-sized helping of that food each day of that week. (Important warning: Never try to reintroduce a food that you already know your child is allergic to. You do not want to risk a serious allergic reaction.) Note each new food in the food diary. If you notice any foods or drinks that provoke the return of bedwetting, withhold those permanently from your child's diet. Any that do not cause relapses can be kept in the diet.

Your allergist will probably recommend that you not keep a child on the starting phase of an elimination diet—with its very limited types of foods—for more than four weeks. If the starting phase produces no results in that time, your allergist may suggest a different assortment of starting foods, or may drop the whole idea.

Other Avenues

There are a few further steps you can take. When you seek the advice of an allergist, on his recommendation you can attempt to eliminate molds, feathers, fur, dander, dust, and/or household chemicals from your child's environment. Such inhalants and other nonfood substances may be the sources of allergies or intolerances.

I hope that this chapter helps you find a cure for your child's bedwetting. However, if you find that neither foods nor other substances contribute to your child's bedwetting, remember that only a minority of children are thought to bedwet because of such allergies and intolerances.

In the following chapters you will learn about some of the more frequent causes of bedwetting, and the next steps you should take in discovering the cause of your child's bedwetting.

8

A NIGHTTIME SHORTAGE OF VASOPRESSIN?

Have you found that your child, although a bedwetter, shows no sign of an urgent need to urinate frequently in the daytime? (See chapter 1 for a complete description of daytime symptoms.) Have you taken your child to a doctor who has found no physical cause of the bedwetting? Have you investigated the possible causes described in the preceding chapters and not found the cause of your child's bedwetting?

If you have observed your child carefully and have seen no daytime frequency, urgency, or spotting of underpants with urine, and if the doctor has found no underlying physical cause, and if you have detected no allergies or food intolerances as causes of the bedwetting, then your child may be bedwetting because her pituitary gland is not producing enough *vasopressin* at night. Vasopressin is a hormone that reduces the output of urine. As V. N. Puri (and many other researchers) have reported, during the night the level of vasopressin increases in nonbedwetting children but decreases in many enuretic children.

FIRST TRY THE WETNESS ALARM SYSTEM

According to Scandinavian researcher Kelm Hjalmas, a wetness alarm system is the first treatment of choice for bedwetting *in children who have no daytime symptoms.* The alarm system works as well as, or better than, other treatments; it is very inexpensive compared to other modes of treatment; and it will not subject your child to a long course of medication. (Wetness alarm systems were discussed in chapter 3.)

95

However, your bedwetter may sleep so heavily that an alarm or vibrator system will not help. If the alarm system fails, there is a drug that may work.

ASK ABOUT DESMOPRESSIN (DDAVP, STIMATE, AND GENERICS)

We have known about the natural hormone vasopressin for some time because an around-the-clock shortage of this hormone causes a disease called diabetes insipidus (different from sugar diabetes; see chapter 4). Researchers experimented with the natural hormone vasopressin but found that if this substance was given in a water solution its action was too short, and if given in an oil solution its action was too long. In addition, both preparations produced unpleasant side effects.

Luckily, in the 1970s, chemists developed a drug called *desmopressin acetate*, which is similar to the natural hormone.

Researchers found that desmopressin (whose trade names are DDAVP and Stimate) was very effective in reducing the enormous urine loss in patients with diabetes insipidus; in addition, the drug caused few side effects. In 1977, S. B. Dimson reported in the journal *Lancet* the use of desmopressin in children with bedwetting.

In 1978, Dr. Marie Birkasova and a group of her colleagues conducted a very careful study on bedwetters who did not have daytime symptoms; they found that 18 of 22 bedwetters were helped by desmopressin. Their report, in *Pediatrics*, speculated that some wetters may not produce enough vasopressin during the night.

Scandinavian doctors Jens P. Nørgaard, E. B. Pedersen, and Jens C. Djurhuus undertook further research, which they reported in 1985 in the *Journal of Urology*; their research confirmed the speculation of the earlier groups. They were also careful to work only with bedwetters who had no daytime urinary symptoms, because in most cases such symptoms indicate other causes of bedwetting.

Later research showed that during the night, bedwetters with a nighttime shortage of vasopressin could excrete as much as four times more urine than the bladder could hold. They had to awaken to urinate or wet the bed.

Many researchers have shown that while children are taking desmopressin, this drug can stop the bedwetting in about 35 percent and can reduce bedwetting in another 35 percent of children who do not have any daytime symptoms or any diseases other than bedwetting. In most cases, bedwetting starts again when the drug is stopped. When the drug is given for a very long period of time (years), some bedwetters stop altogether; however, there is no way of knowing whether the permanent cure stems from the long use of the drug or the passage of time.

WILL MY CHILD RESPOND TO DESMOPRESSIN?

If your child has a nightly shortage of vasopressin, he is likely to respond to desmopressin. Physicians do not usually measure children's vasopressin levels, but if your child seems to produce a great deal of urine at night, you should discuss desmopressin with your doctor. If your child does not produce urine at a greater rate at night than in the daytime, he will probably not respond to desmopressin.

If your child suffers with allergic inflammation of the mucous membrane of the nose (such as hay fever), nasal congestion, or upper respiratory infections, and if the drug is given as a nasal spray, he may not respond because these conditions may interfere with the drug's absorption.

According to researcher H. G. Rushton and associates, your child is likelier to respond to desmopressin if his bladder and bladder capacity are large than if they are small, and if he is in the upper years of childhood rather than a young child. In addition, the fewer nights per week he wets, the likelier he is to respond.

Another study claims that if your child has a significant family history of bedwetting he will be more likely to respond to the drug.

You will know quickly if your child is responsive to the drug: The effect will be seen within a few days. If your child is responsive, the effect will continue for as long as you continue to give him the drug.

ADMINISTRATION AND COST

Desmopressin comes in a "squeeze and squirt" bottle. At bedtime you squirt it into your child's nose, where it is absorbed through the mucous membranes. The dosage varies because its effectiveness is different from child to child; however, a typical starting dose is two squirts; if this dose is not effective, the doctor may increase it to four squirts.

Until very recently, desmopressin was not given by mouth because much of it was destroyed in the gastrointestinal tract. As of this writing, a newly developed tablet form has become available. The tablet will be helpful if your child has nasal congestion or inflammation, or if the spray causes nasal irritation. Researchers Arne Stenberg and Goran Lackgren of Sweden found that the tablet is at least as effective as the spray and may be more effective. However, use of the tablets requires a dose ten times larger than the dose of nasal spray.

Desmopressin is expensive: The cost of a squeeze bottle varies (at this time) from a low of about $80 dollars for a generic preparation to a high of up to about $140 for a brand-name preparation. With a two-squirt regimen, a bottle lasts for about 25 days, less than a month. If your doctor prescribes desmopressin for your child, be sure to "shop around" by calling a number of pharmacies for their prices. (Calls to three pharmacies in one area revealed a substantial difference in cost of the DDAVP brand, ranging from $119 to $140.) The cost of the tablets is about the same as that of the spray bottle.

SAFETY AND SIDE EFFECTS

Desmopressin spray has been in use for more than 30 years and has been found to be generally safe. Mild side effects, which have been reported in fewer than 9 percent of cases, include nasal irritation, nosebleed, nausea, and mild abdominal pain. In addition, the spray contains an ingredient that may cause allergic skin reactions in some children.

Studies by Stenberg and Lackgren, as well as by other researchers, show that the new tablet formulation of desmopressin is also generally safe and does not cause the nasal irritation caused by the spray.

According to Kelm Hjalmas and Bengt Bengtsson of Sweden, and many other researchers, the strong antidiuretic action of desmospressin poses one serious risk: a serious condition called "water intoxication," which causes a type of seizure. You must be especially careful if your child has a tendency to drink a great deal of water, which would add greatly to the risk of water intoxication. When a child who has a high fluid intake receives a dose of desmopressin, the water does not leave the body, and the concentration of salt can be lowered dangerously.

You will know that your child has developed water intoxication if she stops urinating, vomits, rolls her eyes, becomes comatose (unconscious), and possibly suffers convulsions. You must get her quickly to a hospital. There she will respond quickly to treatment with intravenous sodium. There have not been many reported cases of water intoxication, and there have not been any reported fatalities from it.

To guard against water intoxication, the manufacturers of the DDAVP brand of desmopressin recommend that you minimize your child's fluid intake for at least 2 hours before giving the medication and for 8 hours afterward. (The effect of desmopressin can last for up to 12 hours, so some researchers recommend minimizing intake of liquids for 12 hours after giving the medication.) They also advise against drinking beverages that contain caffeine (coffee, tea, hot chocolate, chocolate milk, colas, and many other soda pops).

It has been found that children who have cystic fibrosis should not be treated with desmopressin.

You should not give desmopressin together with certain other drugs, as you will learn from your physician in greater detail. A physician must prescribe desmopressin and monitor its use; never try using another child's desmopressin "just to see if it works."

SIGNIFICANCE OF DESMOPRESSIN

Despite its cost and the requirement for long use, the development and use of desmopressin represent a great advance in the treatment of bedwetting, not only because it gives many bedwetters a relatively safe drug to keep their beds dry, but also because it has spurred a new interest among investigators with regard to the physical causes of bedwetting. It has helped to show that long-term bedwetting from birth is caused by physical problems rather than psychological ones. This understanding has been a long and tragic time in coming.

9

ABNORMALITIES IN THE LOWER URINARY TRACT

If your child is a primary enuretic (bedwetter since birth) who also shows symptoms of urinary problems in the daytime, such as frequent urination, immediate urgency ("rushing to the bathroom"), and spotting or wetting, then one of the most likely causes of both the bedwetting and the daytime symptoms is a small obstruction in your child's urethra. (See chapter 1 for the complete description of daytime urinary symptoms.)

In this chapter I will help you sidestep some common myths, meet real anatomical problems, and understand how small defects lead to bedwetting. I will also discuss the methods of treating these anatomical defects.

For you to understand this chapter, you need some knowledge of the organs of the lower urinary tract, of the way they work together, and of some physical problems that can affect the way they work—as explained in chapter 2. Be sure to read chapter 2, if you haven't already done so, before continuing ahead.

Also, before acting upon this chapter, you should have read and followed the procedures suggested in preceding chapters to rule out other causes of bedwetting and daytime urinary symptoms. Ask yourself these questions: Has your child's pediatrician, family doctor, or specialist examined your child? Has the physician ruled out or treated diabetes, sickle-cell anemia, pinworms, hyperactivity disorder, sleep apnea, or diseased tonsils or adenoids? Has he ruled out or treated any ongoing problem of constipation, encopresis, hemorrhoids, inflamed foreskin, or other inflammations of the genital or anal area? In addition, have you tried to detect and treat allergies and intolerances to foods and other substances? All of these are other causes of bedwetting in children who also show daytime urinary symptoms. If your child is taking medications for epilepsy or asthma, have you asked your doctor to substitute other medications for a while to see if the medications were causing the bedwetting?

If these other possible causes have been ruled out, or if your child's doctor has treated one or more of the problems discussed above but your child is still enuretic, you are ready to investigate causes of long-term bedwetting (from infancy) that originate in the urinary tract.

MISCONCEPTIONS ABOUT BEDWETTING AND DAYTIME URINARY PROBLEMS

You, like many parents, may be troubled by common misconceptions about the causes of your child's bedwetting and daytime urinary symptoms. Because a surprising number of doctors and other health professionals subscribe to these misconceptions, it is important for you to be aware of them and to protect your child from them. Some of the most disturbing ones follow.

Psychological Causes

As you have learned from all you have read in this book so far, your child's primary (since birth), long-term bedwetting and daytime urinary problems are certainly caused by *physical* factors, not by psychological ones. How tragic that so many children with primary urinary problems are still being hurt by the myth that they are wetting because they are unhappy, insecure, hostile, lazy, or seeking attention. And how sad that so many parents (especially mothers) are still being accused of causing their children's urinary problems, either by creating emotional difficulties or by failing to toilet train "properly." Even urologists perpetuate this myth.

For example, the mother of a girl who suffered from both bedwetting and daytime enuresis wrote to me about such an experience:

I took [my daughter] . . . to a urologist, who told me, *without benefit of examination*, that her problem is psychological!

He asked her to promise to be a good girl and never wet her pants again. She promised, of course, and then wet her pants on the way home. . . . His theory was that she was doing it for attention . . . and that it was all our fault for being too lenient with her toilet training—and that children are like puppies and must sometimes be spanked, etc. . . .

If your doctor suggests psychological causes for your child's primary bedwetting and daytime symptoms, be confident that he is wrong—that the causes are physical—and seek another doctor.

Brain Injury

For years doctors thought that children wet the bed persistently because of brain injury or brain disease. We know now that this is a fallacy. Your child does not wet the bed because of an injured or diseased brain.

The mistaken thinking arose from the use of a test called the "Bender-Gestalt Test," which indicated the child's degree of ability to copy simple patterns, and use of brain wave tracings (electroencephalograms, also known as EEGs) rather than use of X rays or neurological studies. X rays and neurological studies almost always show no neurological causes for bedwetting. The ability of EEGs to detect brain disease other than epilepsy remains questionable.

In fact, EEGs may not even be accurate for epilepsy. In some cases they have shown epileptic patterns in children who are light-years away from epilepsy. They often show "immaturity" when no one knows what that really means or how it is supposed to cause bedwetting. One can hardly expect much from a study that records currents from only about one-quarter of the convoluted outer portion of the brain surface and virtually nothing from centers inside the brain. As two-time Pulitzer Prize-winning science writer John Franklin said in 1987 (in his book *Molecules of the Mind*), "One might as well try to deduce the function and purpose of a computer by monitoring the electrical disturbances produced around the outside of the terminal."

Furthermore, EEGs have been around for more than 50 years, and experts still cannot agree on what results are "normal."

According to Canadian neurologist Adrian R. M. Upton, many factors can affect an EEG, including sweats, people walking in the area, and public paging systems. In the ultimate put-down of EEGs (reported in *Medical Tribune* by correspondent Harriet Page), Upton performed an EEG on a blob of lime Jell-O that the EEG found to be "alive."

On the other hand, even if a brain injury or disease *is* present, it does not necessarily follow that this causes bedwetting. I recall an outstanding example:

A mother consulted my former partner, Dr. Ginsburg, because her nine-year-old son, who had a fairly large brain tumor, was very much upset by bedwetting. All of the boy's previous physicians had attributed the bedwetting to the brain tumor. But Dr. Ginsburg questioned the mother carefully and finally learned that the boy had been wetting the bed even before he developed the tumor. Simple urological treatment cured the bedwetting and made life more bearable for the boy.

Urinary Infection

Urinary infection does occur in 20 percent to 30 percent of bedwetting girls, but rarely in boys. If your child has a urinary infection, it must be treated, of course, but the infection may not be a principal cause of bedwetting, as many doctors believe, but simply another result of the underlying anatomical problem, as I suspect.

In 1972 a research group headed by Betty Jones reported in the *Canadian Medical Association Journal* the results of their study of 89 girls who suffered with recurring urinary infections. They found that 56 of these girls also wet their beds. However, treatment that cured the urinary infections cured only 16 of the 56 girls of their bedwetting. In other words, curing the infection in the urine did not stop most of the bedwetting. In light of the results of this study and other studies, it seems that urinary infection by itself is not a principal cause of bedwetting.

If both the urinary infection and the bedwetting are caused by the same underlying physical problem, then treating the urinary infection alone will most likely not cure your child's bedwetting. You must make sure that the physician treats the underlying physical problem, too.

The "Unstable" Bladder

Be very skeptical if a doctor tells you that your child bedwets because of an "unstable bladder." The "unstable bladder" is one of the numerous terms used by many doctors to describe a bladder that supposedly contracts (and expels urine) inappropriately. It is said to cause urgency, frequent urination, inability to control urine, and bedwetting. Unfortunately, by overrating the role of the bladder and ignoring the role of the urethra in producing urinary problems, too many doctors fail to treat the physical defects that cause both the bedwetting and the daytime problems.

The "unstable bladder" has been blamed on psychological disturbances, nervous system defects, and other things. However, except for diseases of the nervous system, the only known cause of an "unstable bladder" is something that obstructs the outflow, as Anthony R. Mundy noted in a review of the subject published in *Urologic Clinics of North America*.

In other words, the problem is in the urethra, not in the bladder. As researcher Stig Karlson showed in a report in the *Scandinavian Journal of Obstetrics and Gynecology*, urine entering the urethra even when the bladder is totally relaxed can produce the urgent need to urinate. And as L. Penders and associates found and reported in *European Urology*, instead of an unstable bladder, we need to think about an unstable urethra. Doctors need to deal with the urethral abnormalities that trigger inappropriate voiding reflexes.

If a urologist blames your child's bedwetting and daytime urinary problems on an "unstable bladder," you ought to look for another urologist—one who understands the role of urethral abnormalities in the cause of bedwetting.

Bladder-Sphincter "Disharmony"

In recent years some investigators have blamed bedwetting and daytime urinary problems on a "disharmony" between the bladder and the voluntary urinary muscles. They say, in other words, that the voluntary muscles fail to relax during urination as they normally should. They blame the supposed "failure to relax" on many things, including improper toilet training, immaturity, and efforts to stop "irritable bladder" contractions.

It appears, however, that the tests used to detect the muscle spasm or tightening may actually *cause* it. Youngsters, surrounded by strangers, hooked up to mysterious instruments, and anxious about what is going on, will react with muscle-tightening apprehension and tension, particularly in the part of the anatomy where the tests are being conducted.

The diagnosis remains difficult and misleading. In 1981 the International Continence Society, a worldwide organization of doctors and scientists devoted to the problems of urinary control, advised against making this diagnosis except in cases where there is obvious spinal cord disease (which can cause this disharmony). However, spinal cord disease is extremely rare in bedwetters.

Nevertheless, some of this testing still takes place. If a doctor recommends that your child undergo tests to detect "bladder-sphincter disharmony," you would be wise to refuse them.

VERY SMALL ABNORMALITIES OF THE URETHRA

Many children who have the daytime symptoms of frequent and urgent urination (discussed in chapter 1) wet their beds. Other children who have daytime symptoms sleep so lightly that they awaken to go to the toilet several times each night. Many of the children in both of these groups have one *or sometimes more than one* abnormality of the urethra. These urethral abnormalities range from very small and subtle ones to large and obvious ones. However, most often they are small and seemingly insignificant, to the point where some radiologists and urologists who examine the X-ray photographs sometimes mistakenly overlook them and report conditions to be "normal."

These abnormalities, even the small and subtle ones, create problems that can cause or contribute to your child's bedwetting, as I have reported extensively (along with many others) in the medical literature. Another physician who found that these small abnormalities can cause bedwetting and daytime urinary symptoms, and who contributed enormously to what is known about them and their treatment, is the renowned physician W. Hardy Hendren III, who was the chief of pediatric surgical service at Boston's Children's Hospital for 22 years and later was the chief of surgery at Massachusetts General Hospital in Boston. For his contributions, Dr. Hendren was honored with many awards, including the Pediatric Urology Medal from the Urology Section of the American Academy of Pediatrics.

Urethral Abnormalities in Girls

As you saw in chapter 2, the girl's urethra is much shorter than the boy's and therefore is subject to fewer types of abnormalities than the boy's. In a girl the most likely urethral abnormalities are either an opening to the outside ("nozzle") that is too narrow or a "nozzle" that doesn't open sufficiently for the flow.

In either of these defects, the opening is too narrow for the flow, which results in high pressure on the urethral walls inside the urethra. This pressure causes the urethral walls, with their involuntary muscles, to become forced apart (dilatated) and weakened, so they are less able to hold urine. (See chapter 2, figure 2.6.) The pressure and turbulence of the flow also inflame the urethral walls. The irritated nerve endings in these inflamed walls then tend to trigger sudden voiding reflexes that are difficult or impossible to control.

Urethral Abnormalities in Boys

In boys (as in girls) the most common defect is an opening at the nozzle end of the urethra that is too small for the flow of urine. Some doctors may overlook the opening as a cause of bedwetting in certain children because the opening may not "appear" small, or because its measured size may be within "the normal range." However, an opening of one size may be adequate in one child but inadequate in another, depending on the pressure of the child's urinary flow.

An additional defect common to boys is a *narrowing* or *constriction* a little way behind the opening or somewhere farther back in the urethra. Unfortunately, some boys have more than one of these narrowings. (Generally, a narrowing is something a boy is born with, although some narrowings can be caused by injury.)

Still another abnormality among boys is a *flap* or *fold* inside the urethra at the point where the back section of the urethra meets the middle section. Such a flap or fold can be very small (and difficult for the doctor to detect), or it can be large and easily detected; however, in any size, it can partially block the flow of urine. During urination, the larger folds fan out or balloon out, causing even more blockage. Any obstruction causes pressure that produces inflammation and irritated nerve endings in the urethra while pushing apart and weakening the urethral walls. (Many doctors refer to urethral flaps and folds as *valves*, but they are not valves in the true sense. Urologists have been aware of the larger "valves" for a long time but have generally ignored the more subtle ones.)

If your son has a problem in his urethra, it is most likely only one small abnormality. However, it may be more than one. Some boys have two or even three small defects in the urethra.

How Urethral Abnormalities Cause Wetting

How can small abnormalities, which are seemingly so minor that many doctors consider them normal or insignificant, cause or contribute to your child's urinary symptoms and bedwetting?

From long experience in treating this type of bedwetting and from extensive study in this area, I have developed the following picture of what happens. Bladder and urethral flow (hydrodynamics) exist in a very delicate balance that is easily upset. The slightest obstruction in your child's urethra, even a small fraction of an inch, significantly increases *pressure* and *turbulence* (churning) of the flow during urination. This pressure and turbulence, in turn, inflame the lining of the urethra. The inflammation then produces abnormal pressure on nerve endings in the urethra, resulting in hair-trigger reflexes to urinate.

In addition, the increased side pressure pushes apart and weakens the involuntary muscles of the urethral walls and, to some extent, the muscles of the bladder neck. All of these muscles, as you saw in chapter 2, have the job of holding back urine without our being aware of it. When they are weakened, so is their ability to hold back urine.

Before the bladder is full enough to require normal urination, the weakened bladder-neck muscles allow some urine to seep into the urethra; this starts a reflex to urinate that occurs without your child's awareness. In other words, it causes the urethra to open before it should and the bladder to contract (and expel urine) before it should. Normally, as the bladder fills, the urinary sphincters automatically tighten to prevent urinating, and the bladder remains relaxed to receive more urine. However, if the pressure within the urethra increases beyond a certain point, the urethra automatically tends to relax, which in turn causes the bladder to begin contracting and expelling urine, without your child having any control over the process.

When the urethra opens—and causes the bladder to contract before it should—your child may experience a sensation of urine passing along the urethra or of some urine loss. In response, your child quickly tightens the voluntary muscles that surround the urethra. Normally this would close the urethra. However, when the voluntary muscles and the pelvic floor muscles squeeze an irritated urethra, they cause abnormally high pressures that quickly change the muscle reflex that would normally *hold* the urine into a reflex that *expels* it. Under these circumstances, the harder your child tries to stop the outflow, the more she tends to bring it on.

Faced with such an emergency, your child will reinforce her sphincter muscles by tightening the muscles between her legs, crossing her thighs or squeezing them together, sitting on her heels, or clutching her genitals. These actions delay the reflex to urinate for a brief time, but they do not stop it. If your child does not hurry to the bathroom, or if someone pushes her out of her sphincter-reinforcing position, she is likely to have a wetting "accident."

All of this helps to explain why, during the day, affected children press their hands to their genital areas, spot their underpants, rush to the bathroom, and urinate frequently. But why do they wet the bed?

During sleep, the voluntary muscles of the body relax, which is why we cannot sleep standing up. The voluntary muscles of the pelvic floor and the voluntary muscles that surround the urethra relax. As Ian Oswald noted in his book *Sleeping and Waking*, the deeper the sleep, the greater the degree of relaxation of these muscles. Your heavily sleeping child cannot exert the control she has during the day. If the bladder neck is weak or dilatated, relaxation of the voluntary muscles and pelvic floor muscles results in some urine entering the urethra before the bladder fills. The entrance of urine into the urethra, you remember, leads to a sudden reflex to urinate. The bladder contracts, and urination begins. Your heavily sleeping child is not aware of it and cannot stop it. On the other hand, if sleep is not too deep and the voluntary muscles have not relaxed sufficiently to allow urine to enter the urethra, your child will awaken to urinate. Of course, severe irritation of the urethra or severe weakness of the bladder-neck muscles can cause wetting even when your child is sleeping lightly or, in some cases, when she is fully awake.

Heavy Sleep Contributes to Bedwetting Caused by Urethral Defects

As you learned in chapter 3, the majority of children who bedwet, no matter what the principal cause of the wetting, are unusually heavy sleepers, very difficult to awaken. It is because of this inability to awaken that many bedwetters cannot respond when the reflex to urinate is triggered. Also, the heavier the sleep, the more the voluntary muscles relax and allow the urine to enter the urethra, triggering the bedwetting episode. Children who have the same physical problems as bedwetters but who do not wet their beds are much lighter sleepers; they are able to awaken each time the reflex to urinate is triggered. (If you haven't already read chapter 3, which discusses the role of heavy sleep in bedwetting, be sure to familiarize yourself with it before reading ahead.)

UROLOGICAL EXAMINATIONS

If all other causes have been ruled out, or if potential causes have been found and treated but the bedwetting and daytime symptoms continue, then your child needs to be examined by a *urologist*—a medical doctor who specializes in treating urinary/genital problems.

Some of the sections that follow contain more detail than you were probably expecting. However, you will have an advantage if you are well informed—if you know what to expect and also what to avoid.

The Preliminary Examination

When you take your child to a urologist, you will be asked to provide a history of your child's problems. Then the urologist will do a physical examination focused mainly on your child's symptoms and on any physical problems that may relate to the urinary system.

The urologist will palpate or tap on the child's abdomen to discover if the bladder is perhaps not emptying properly, and inspect the genital and anal areas carefully to check for a number of possible contributions to bedwetting, such as hemorrhoids, inflammation of the genital or anal area, and pinworms. (A method you can use at home to see if your child has pinworms was described in chapter 5.) The urologist will also check the rectum to detect whether stool is being retained. (Normally the rectum does not retain stool until the child feels the need to defecate. Retention of stool in the rectum could be the cause of your child's bedwetting, as discussed in chapter 6.) In addition, the urologist will look at your child's lower spine and test your child's reflexes and nervous system responses to see if any abnormality of the lower spine (such as spina bifida) could be contributing to the bedwetting. (If there is a problem in any of these areas, it must be addressed before the doctor can make any further recommendations.)

If possible, the urologist will watch your child urinate. The shape and speed of the flow can indicate urethral abnormalities. In a boy, the stream normally flares (has an oval shape with a clear center as it leaves the penis). If the stream is fast and straight (has no oval shape), it indicates that the urethral opening (at the front of the penis) is too narrow. (See figure 9-1.) In addition, your child's urine will be tested for sugar

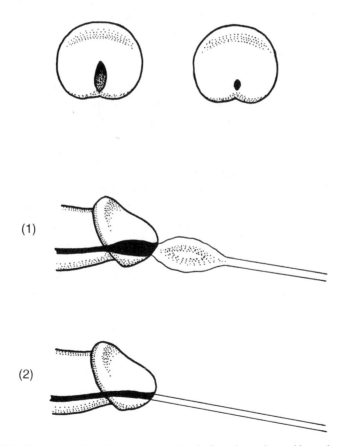

Figure 9.1. The shape of the urinary stream as it exits from the penis provides a clue to the condition of the urethral opening. (1) The normal opening produces an exiting stream that contains a flare with a translucent center. (2) The narrowed opening produces a jet stream.

(diabetes), bacteria (infection), and specific gravity (ability of the kidneys to concentrate urine).

X Rays of the Kidneys

The *kidneys* are organs that process urine. The great majority of bedwetting children have normal kidneys and don't require kidney X rays. The urologist should suggest kidney X rays only if he has reason to believe there may be a problem in that area. If your child has pain in the kidney areas or pus in the urine, and if the urologist suspects a kidney problem, he will request that you make an appointment for your child to see a radiologist to obtain an *intravenous pyelogram (IVP)*.

To conduct an IVP, the radiologist must inject a special inert fluid called a "radioopaque" fluid into a vein in the child's arm. This fluid, which shows up on X rays, travels through the bloodstream to the kidneys, where it is excreted like urine. The radiologist or a technician will take a number of X-ray pictures as the fluid passes though the child's urinary tract. These pictures will clearly outline the kidneys, the ureters (tubes that lead from the kidneys to the bladder), and the bladder itself. If your child must undergo an IVP, which is almost always performed in the morning, he should not eat breakfast nor drink anything that morning until the procedure is completed.

The IVP should be avoided unless the urologist suspects kidney disease because it has several drawbacks: It exposes the child to the radiation involved in a number of X-ray pictures; and when radioopaque fluid is injected into the bloodstream, it causes allergic reactions in a few children. Children also find the experience frightening, especially when they are injected with the radioopaque fluid and are faced with the X-ray equipment. If your urologist requests that you make an appointment for an IVP, you should ask for his reasons for the request.

X Rays of the Bladder and Urethra—
Conscious Voiding Cystourethrogram

Although bedwetting children rarely need X rays of the kidneys, they usually need X rays of the bladder and urethra. These, too, must be scheduled and taken by a radiologist.

Many urologists require that these X rays be taken while the child is urinating, in a procedure called a *conscious voiding cystourethrogram.* In this procedure, the radiologist passes a catheter (a tiny tube) through the urethra to the bladder (the tube is so tiny, it rarely causes the child more than temporary physical discomfort, but you can ask the radiologist to use a local anesthetic to avoid any physical discomfort). Then she fills the bladder with the fluid that shows up on X-ray pictures. (When the fluid is sent directly into the bladder rather than through the bloodstream, there is less danger of allergic reactions.)

Then the radiologist monitors the process by means of a fluoroscope (an instrument that allows the viewer to see X-ray images of the body directly, rather than by photography) and also takes several X-ray photos while the child urinates. The pictures show any abnormal backing up of urine (reflux) to the kidneys, abnormal size of the bladder, and abnormal (enlarged) bladder muscle. They also reveal any pushing apart of the urethral walls, areas of narrowing at the bladder neck, and narrowings (called *strictures*) inside the urethra.

I do not favor the conscious voiding cystourethrogram for several reasons. The procedure is very scary for children. Frightened children do not urinate normally for the study, especially after the catheter is inserted. Also, the fluoroscoping and each X-ray photo exposes the child to X-ray radiation. Because of the fluoroscoping and the number of pictures required in this procedure, the child is exposed to considerable radiation. At the same time, the conscious voiding cystourethrogram often fails to reveal small urethral abnormalities. And the procedure is expensive.

If your urologist requests this procedure, you may want to ask him about the possibility of skipping the conscious voiding study and doing the unconscious study (described next) after your child is under anesthesia. The unconscious study spares the child the considerable stress of the conscious study.

Unconscious Static Cystourethrography: A Way to X-Ray the Bladder and Urethra Without Terrifying the Child

Because of the limitations of the conscious voiding cystourethrogram, some urologists use a different procedure, the one I prefer. In our experience with almost three thousand children, my colleague Dr. Ginsburg and I learned that we do not have to perform expensive testing, and we do not have to frighten and stress conscious children with insertion of the catheter and fluid, along with all the other procedures involved in obtaining X-ray photos of the urethra and bladder.

If other conditions and diseases have been ruled out (or corrected) and the continued bedwetting is accompanied by daytime urinary symptoms, we are reasonably sure that there is a problem in the urethra that will require hospitalization, anesthesia, and surgery. We then recommend that the child be hospitalized for further examination and treatment. At the hospital, with the child under anesthesia, we perform *unconscious static cystourethrography*.

This procedure involves passing a small catheter to the bladder; filling the bladder with the fluid that shows on X rays; pulling out the catheter; and taking only one X-ray picture as the elastic or rubberbandlike rebound of the bladder drives the fluid through the urethra and out. This procedure is preferable because it causes the child far less stress, and with only one X-ray picture and no fluoroscoping required, it exposes the child to much less radiation. In addition, as Dr. Roger Berg (a radiologist) and I reported in the *Journal of Urology*, this method is better than the conscious voiding method for diagnostic purposes.

There are additional benefits to this method. While the child is still under anesthesia, we can also examine the urethra and bladder with a cystourethroscope, an important procedure (described in the next section) that cannot be performed without general anesthesia.

At the same time, when we find the abnormality within the urethra, we can immediately perform the simple surgery needed to correct it, and then, immediately after the surgery, repeat the cystourethrography with one more X-ray picture to see whether the abnormality has been fully corrected (all while the child is under anesthesia). In all, the child is subjected to anesthesia only once, and to only two X-ray photos. Furthermore, the child is spared the physical and psychological distress of consciously experiencing the handling of the genital area, the insertion of the catheter through the urethra, the filling of the bladder, and the expelling of the inserted liquid while photographs are taken. Your child would prefer that method, just as you would yourself.

No one likes to hospitalize a child or submit a child to anesthesia, but without anesthesia, the urologist cannot use a cystourethroscope, nor dilate the urethra, nor perform necessary surgery. Of course, there is a very small risk in anesthesia, as in any medical procedure, but modern anesthesia is very safe. Children are hospitalized and anesthetized for procedures of many types, such as removal of the appendix, adenoids, and so forth, when conditions require them. A defect in the urethra that causes not only bedwetting, but also many other urologically related problems throughout life, is just as serious a condition. As a parent, you would want the best diagnostic procedure, and the best treatment to correct this abnormality, just as in the case of any other serious condition.

Cystourethroscopy

A urologist can examine the urethra and bladder by looking into them through a special instrument called a *cystourethroscope*, which is inserted into the urethra. Through this instrument, urologists can see inflammations of the bladder, enlarged bladder muscles (which indicate that an obstruction has made them work harder), a narrowed bladder neck, inflammation of the lining of the urethra, and obstructions in the urethra such as folds and flaps. Urologists can even take photographs through the cystourethroscope. This instrument comes in several sizes, including very small ones for examining children. The procedure is called *cystourethroscopy*, and it is performed only when the child is under anesthesia.

Bougienage

When the child is under anesthesia for the procedures described above, the urologist can use a very slender instrument called a *bougie* to detect very small urethral narrowings (strictures) that sometimes do not show up on urethral X rays. The bullet-shaped head of the bougie permits it to be inserted easily into the urethra; but as the bougie is slowly withdrawn, the blunt back of the tapered head "catches" on any strictures, even very subtle ones, thus detecting them. The bougie cannot be used without anesthesia.

The use of the bougie is important. It enabled Richards P. Lyon and Donald R. Smith to demonstrate (in the *Journal of Urology*) that obstruction in girls that was thought to be at the bladder neck was actually at the nozzle opening. This discovery has spared many girls from bladder-neck surgery and the incontinence that bladder-neck surgery can sometimes cause. (You will learn more about the reasons for avoiding bladder-neck surgery a little later in this chapter.)

Ultrasound

An increasing number of physicians are using ultrasound as another means of examining bedwetters. (If you are a mother, you may have experienced an ultrasound procedure during your pregnancy.) An outgrowth of sonar used in World War II to detect submarines, ultrasound relies on an echo effect.

In this procedure, a machine generates a series of bursts of ultrasonic energy and focuses them into a beam. The operator of the machine directs the beam into the tissues to be examined. Because tissues vary in density, the echoes they form also vary. The echoes are converted into electrical impulses displayed on a screen, showing abnormalities of size, shape, and structure.

Within the past ten years, new instruments, knowledge, and techniques have greatly increased the diagnostic ability of ultrasound. Without exposing children to the many X rays or intravenous injections of radioopaque fluid that are used in the IVP, doctors can use ultrasound—in many cases—to screen for significant abnormalities of the kidney and bladder (such as enlargement), as well as large urethral abnormalities, the backing up of urine from the bladder to the kidneys (reflux), and urine left in the bladder after urination.

Unfortunately, however, while ultrasound can detect large, obvious flaps and folds in boys' urethras, it can't detect the more subtle flaps, folds, narrowings, and inflammations that result in so much bedwetting. To detect these smaller defects, the urologist needs to use the cystourethroscope, urethrography, and in some cases the bougie. If your urologist goes no farther than the use of ultrasound to detect small urethral abnormalities, you should find a urologist who will conduct the necessary examinations.

Urodynamics

"Urodynamics" is a word that urologists use to describe various methods of measuring bladder pressures, rates of urine flow, sphincter action, and so on. The urodynamic examination most commonly used is the cystometrogram, which means measurement of bladder pressure. I do not recommend this procedure. The test requires the physician to pass a catheter through the urethra into the bladder and to fill the child's bladder (through the catheter) with water or carbon dioxide. A machine called a cystometer, with a connection to the catheter, records the pressures as the amounts of fluid or gas increase. This test is supposed to help the urologist detect abnormalities of volume, pressure, and bladder activity.

The cystometrogram has great limitations. Its results can change from one examination to the next in the same untreated child. The cystometrogram reveals nothing about any obstruction in the urethra. It tells nothing about how the urethra is working. Since the bladder and the urethra do not operate in isolation from one another, the cystometrogram remains at best incomplete, at worst wholly misleading. In my view, it often indicates diseases that do not exist and leads to treatments that do not cure.

Urodynamic testing of children is totally impractical for still another important reason: You cannot get a recently catheterized child, who is hooked up to a machine in a strange and frightening environment, to urinate as she would at home.

For the problem of bedwetting and daytime symptoms in a child who is otherwise healthy, you would be wise to refuse this form of testing.

SURGICAL TREATMENT

If your bedwetting child has any narrowing or obstruction in the urethra that interferes with the normal flow of urine, a simple operation will remove or correct the abnormality. Most urethral abnormalities are easily correctable. Correcting them cures the daytime urinary problems very quickly in about 85 percent of children who undergo the surgery, and cures the bedwetting within four months in about 70 percent. In about 15 percent, the operation cures the daytime problems, but the bedwetting requires additional (nonurological) treatment to overcome excessively heavy sleep (see chapter 3). In any case, the surgical treatment eliminates the principal cause, rather than eliminating only a symptom, and prevents more serious problems (discussed in chapter 1) from developing in later life.

There are several types of surgery that correct different types of defects in the urinary tract.

Meatotomy

If your child's urethral opening to the outside (called the meatus) is too small, the urologist needs to make a small incision to make it larger. This procedure is called a meatotomy, pronounced "mee-ah-tot-oh-mee."

After the incision, the urologist must take steps to block the strong tendency of the cut margins to heal back into their original position. The most effective, least painful method is the one that Dr. Ginsburg and I discovered and reported in the *Journal of Urology*. This method is to apply thin goldleaf to the wound. The goldleaf remains in place for about 10 days until the tissues have healed and cannot grow together again; then the goldleaf falls off by itself. This simple technique removes the need for stitches, reduces operating time, and prevents secondary bleeding.

In the past, doctors instructed mothers to insert a lubricated glass eye-dropper into the opening at least four times a day, until the edges healed open. The eye-dropper method is still in use by some urologists. Most doctors still ask the parent to insert an object such as the tip of an ophthalmic ointment tube into the meatus once or twice a day for a few weeks until healing is complete. These methods (which are not necessary when goldleaf is used) are very stressful for both the parent and the child and are truly undesirable from a psychological point of view. Try to find a doctor who uses the goldleaf method (or who would be willing to try it) or another method less stressful than the daily object-insertion method.

A still older method of preventing the margins from growing together involves the application of 100 percent silver nitrate. Regrettably, a few urologists may still use this very old method. Silver nitrate destroys blood vessels and surrounding tissue, forms a frightening black area, and sometimes fails to keep the cut edges from growing together again. Be sure that this method is not used on your child.

If you know that a meatotomy is necessary, you can discuss in advance with the urologist the method she uses to prevent the margins of the incision from growing together. If one of the older methods is mentioned, you can suggest the goldleaf method. However, be open-minded to new methods: Urologists with any experience may have their own methods perhaps as effective as the use of goldleaf.

Correcting Narrowings, Folds, and Flaps

Sometimes urologists use a simple instrument called a *sound* to stretch narrowings (which doctors call "strictures") in the urethra. For some strictures, however, they need to perform a simple surgical procedure. Either of these procedures requires anesthesia.

A narrowing is different from a fold or flap of tissue (which doctors call "valves"). Where folds or flaps are the problem, one or even two must be removed from within the urethra. After locating their position (with the cystourethroscope and X-ray photo), the urologist easily removes these obstructions with a very slender electrode, which is passed through the cystourethroscope. Figure 9-2 shows a common type of small "valve" (as seen through a cystourethroscope), and the changed area after the removal of the obstruction.

Say "No" to Bladder-Neck Surgery

When a urethral obstruction makes the bladder work harder than it normally does to expel urine, the muscles at the bladder opening or "neck" become larger and interfere with the free flow of urine. This problem has caused some misunderstanding. In the past, some physicians were not aware that the increase in the size of the bladder-neck muscle resulted from an obstruction in the urethra. They cut out part of the bladder-neck muscle to enlarge the bladder opening.

Unfortunately, in males, cutting out part of this muscle weakens the sphincter responsible for preventing semen from shooting back into the

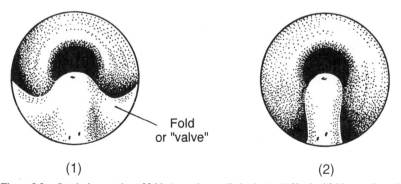

Fold
or "valve"

(1)   (2)

Figure 9.2. Surgical correction of folds (sometimes called valves). (1) Urethral folds seen through a cystourethroscope. (2) View of area after surgical removal of folds by means of cautery.

bladder (instead of along the urethra and out of the body) during sexual climax. While this condition will not usually disturb sexual desire or ability to function later in life, it will cause infertility because the sperm will not reach the partner's womb.

Bladder-neck surgery should almost never be performed on male children. Correcting the urethral obstruction in the child generally solves the problem. In those cases in which the problem is neglected until adult life, many urologists have learned that a simple incision into the adult's enlarged bladder-neck muscle, without removal of any of its substance, solves the problem of the enlarged muscle and greatly reduces the risk of infertility.

The same unfortunate misconception about the neck of the bladder in girls stems from the fact that when a urethral obstruction widens or pushes apart the urethral walls, the bladder neck looks as if it is narrowed. Urologists who mistakenly regarded the bladder neck as narrowed used to cut the bladder neck to make the area larger. This illogical procedure not only overlooked the real cause (a problem in the urethra) but also endangered the girl's ability to hold urine. If a doctor wants to cut or enlarge the neck of your daughter's bladder, refuse it. Be sure to get a second opinion quickly!

Success of Surgery

What are the results of the correct surgery to widen narrowings and/or to remove folds or flaps in the urethra? Soon after surgery, children urinate with lower pressures and, in the great majority of cases, with very little discomfort.

As I reported in *Urology* and in *Postgraduate Medicine* (and as many others reported, including David Mahony, J. Vanwaenbergh, Yoshimori Mori, K. Haubensak, and K. M. Schrott), within days or weeks of the correct surgery, the daytime urinary symptoms in approximately 85 percent of the cases disappear or become significantly reduced; and within four months, bedwetting in approximately 70 percent of the cases stops or becomes significantly reduced. (All of my results, and those of Dr. Ginsburg, were independently reviewed and confirmed by Dr. Robert Ambrose, urologist, and Dr. John Stockman, chief of the department of urology, at Morristown Memorial Hospital, Morristown, New Jersey.)

What about the 15 percent of bedwetters whose daytime symptoms have been corrected but who are still bedwetting four months later? At this point, most of them can be cured successfully with urine alarm systems that overcome the heavy sleep problem (see chapter 3), although that method would not have worked before the surgical correction. Some are reportedly cured with two or three months of treatment with imipramine (Tofranil). (However, if your urologist prescribes imipramine for your child, you must follow the prescribed dosage instructions carefully, because overdosing with imipramine can cause severe side effects or even death.)

Although in most cases of urethral obstruction only one (often subtle) abnormality is present, it is possible for two or as many as three abnormalities to be present. For example, there could be a "nozzle" opening that is too small, along with another narrowing just behind it, and a flap or fold of tissue farther back. If all are removed at the same time, the operation will achieve its results and your child will not experience pain after the operation.

This is extremely important. If one of the defects, no matter how subtle, is left untreated, not only will the urinary problem remain, but also the child may experience a significant amount of pain in the healing period after surgery. I have treated patients who remembered enormous postoperative pain that resulted from a previous surgeon's treatment that failed to remove all of the existing obstructions. (Fortunately, this is a rare event when the surgery is performed by urologists who are alert to subtle abnormalities.)

Thus, in selecting a urologist, you will want to look for one who does not dismiss subtle folds or flaps as "insignificant," which, unfortunately, many urologists do. And if your child experiences pain and discomfort after the operation, you will need to bring him back to the urologist for further examination and treatment.

Caution is necessary in selecting a urologist. However, from my long years of successful treatment of bedwetters, I can say with assurance that for bedwetters who have urethral obstructions, no matter how small and subtle, the surgical measures I advocate provide the highest rate of cures with the lowest rate of recurrences. A significant number of other urologists have reported similar results.

I urge you to discuss your child's urinary problems at length first with your pediatrician or family physician. If you decide to visit a urologist, you have the right to know beforehand the urologist's views on bedwetting, the treatment methods he uses, and the results he obtains. You can ask the pediatrician if he knows the views of the urologist he recommends to you. Or you can telephone the urologist to ask him about his methods and his success rates.

You should be wary of urologists who say that they seldom find small physical abnormalities, such as the abnormalities described in this chapter, in the urethras of those bedwetting children who also have daytime urinary symptoms. Such urologists will dismiss as "insignificant" the small and subtle abnormalities that I (and many others) have found to be such important causes of bedwetting. And these physicians will seldom contribute to the cure of bedwetting.

Will the Hospital Experience Be Frightening for Your Child?

We were as concerned as you are about the effect of hospitalization on children, so Dr. Ginsburg and I made a study of parents' estimates of their children's reactions to hospitalization. We gathered their responses from an extensive follow-up questionnaire we gave to parents of each child on whom we performed surgery.

Parents reported, with very few exceptions, that their children who were properly prepared for the experience were not intimidated by it. (See chapter 10 for suggestions on how to prepare your child for doctor visits and hospital stays.) Many of the children were even proud of going to the hospital for "their operation." (Perhaps the glamor of television shows about hospitals helps to promote a positive attitude.) Parents confided that their children were very anxious to be "cured" of their bedwetting and were deeply grateful to be taken seriously.

A RARE CONDITION: THE "LAZY" BLADDER

Although the chances are very small that your child may have the unusual condition called the "lazy" bladder, I do not want to omit it from mention, because it does contribute to bedwetting. It is a condition in which the bladder is exceptionally large. This large, thin-muscled bladder is almost always associated with a large, thin-muscled rectum. Often a parent has the same condition, so I believe that it is inherited and exists in the child from birth.

Normally, children who have this condition have no symptoms except that they go to the bathroom far less frequently than other children. They toilet train very early, and they are good travelers, probably because of their large bladders.

However, because these children void so infrequently, bacteria have an opportunity to multiply and build up, causing urinary infections. During infections, children experience urinary urgency and frequency during the daytime, as well as bedwetting or a number of trips to the bathroom at night.

If your child shows this group of symptoms, she should be examined by a urologist. The condition needs to be treated first with antibiotics to fight the infection. Then your child needs to be trained to go to the bathroom to urinate every two hours (approximately) instead of waiting for the signal that her bladder is full.

TWO UNUSUAL DAYTIME CONDITIONS

Most children who have daytime urinary symptoms also wet the bed, or if they are light sleepers, get up several times during the night to urinate. However, there are two conditions that produce some daytime symptoms without producing bedwetting or frequent nighttime urinating. Because they can be confused with other problems discussed in this chapter, I will describe them.

Giggle Incontinence

A condition called *giggle incontinence* is rare, but I have seen children who have had it.

With "giggle incontinence," a child experiences sudden, involuntary emptying of the bladder during a bout of laughter. Children who have this condition are usually preadolescent girls, but sometimes boys, and sometimes young adults. They have no control over it. The cause is still unknown. We know that the condition generally disappears with the passage of time in most but not all cases.

There is no generally accepted treatment, although researchers J. T. Brockelbank and S. R. Meadow of the United Kingdom reported curing two boys with use of the drug propantheline; P. K. Sher reported (in *Pediatric Neurology*) successful treatment with the drug methylphenidate; and M. G. Arena and a group of Italian researchers reported curing a girl with the use of imipramine (Tofranil).

If your child is experiencing giggle incontinence, reassure her that it will probably go away before she is an adult and that you know she can't help it. She may want to carry a waterproof bag for wet garments, and a change of underwear and other clothing. Sanitary pads and/or adult diapers (such as Depends) worn under clothing may be helpful.

Extraordinary Daytime Frequency Syndrome

In extraordinary daytime frequency syndrome, which doctors also call *pollakiuria*, children who have had no urinary difficulties suddenly begin urinating very frequently—some as often as every 5 to 15 minutes. In most cases, the children (who are mostly boys) do not wet their beds and do not need to urinate during the night. Urine cultures and examinations show no infections or other physical problems. The syndrome lasts for only days, weeks, or months (although one reported case continued intermittently for $3^1/2$ years). It stops by itself.

Among other researchers, Jeri Zoubek and colleagues, and Lee W. Bass, who described it in separate issues of the journal *Pediatrics*, advised against treating this condition with drugs. However, in a letter to the same journal, urologist Arnold H. Colodny suggested that imipramine (Tofranil) could break the cycle or alleviate the symptoms.

The cause of daytime urinary frequency syndrome is unknown. Researchers A. K. Gupta and colleagues, who studied 10 boys who experienced this syndrome, reported in the journal *Indian Pediatrics* that 7 of the boys developed it after an upper respiratory infection. Bass, who studied 13 children, reported that the condition developed in 10 of the children after they had experienced very significant psychological stressors.

If your child is suffering from this unusual condition and his doctor can find no infection or other physical cause, you need to offer sympathy and reassurance that the condition is temporary. You should explore and discuss with your child any threatening or stressful situations he may be experiencing. And if the need to urinate is so frequent that it is disrupting your child's life, you may want to ask the doctor to try treatment with imipramine. (Remember that you must supervise use of this drug very carefully.)

10

PREPARING YOUR CHILD FOR MEDICAL EXPERIENCES AND SURGICAL PROCEDURES

Your search for the cause of your child's bedwetting will begin with a visit to your child's pediatrician and may progress to an examination by a specialist. I hope that one of these physicians will find or confirm the underlying cause and begin successful treatment of it. However, the specialist may find a need for special testing, and then, perhaps, a surgical procedure.

At each step of the way, it is important for you to help prepare your child for what to expect. You must share information, dispel fears, and correct misconceptions. At the same time, you need to prepare yourself, as well as to gather information for the physicians so they can make informed diagnoses. This chapter will assist you in these efforts.

PREPARING TO GO TO THE DOCTOR

When to Start Seeking a Doctor's Help

If your child has been wetting since birth, don't worry about it until he is four or five years of age, when he should be examined by his pediatrician or family doctor, who will begin investigating the causes. However, if your child also has been experiencing either frequent bowel symptoms or the need to urinate frequently or urgently in the daytime, he should be examined as soon as you are aware of the problem. Of course, if your child has unexplained fever, abdominal or back pain, inflammation of the genital or anal area, persistent excessive thirst, or signs of pinworms (such as scratching the anal area), he should be examined immediately.

If your child has been dry for some time (about six months or longer) but then started bedwetting again, observe him carefully. If he has no fever, no daytime urinary symptoms, and seems otherwise normal and well, you can wait a week to see the doctor; the wetting may be a temporary episode that will resolve itself quickly. However, if he has symptoms of urinary frequency and urgency in the daytime, his new wetting may be the result of a flare-up of whatever is causing the daytime symptoms; you should make an appointment with the doctor. Certainly, if your child has a fever or any of the signs of illness described in the previous paragraph, he should be seen by the doctor immediately.

Select a Doctor

It is important for your child to have not only a competent doctor but also a kindly and communicative one. To investigate bedwetting, the doctor must examine and probe many parts of the body, including parts that the child rightfully considers very private; there must be rapport between doctor and patient. If past experience shows that your child's pediatrician or family doctor is stern, cold, distant, or uncommunicative, this is the time for you to ask for recommendations from other parents in your area and make a change. Among other qualities you should look for in your child's doctor is flexibility: Ask if he is willing to consider and investigate all possibilities. In addition, you want a doctor who does not dismiss or minimize the problem of bedwetting but who shows an active interest in discovering the underlying cause or causes. The National Kidney Foundation maintains a nationwide referral service to help people find local pediatricians, family doctors, and urologists who have indicated an interest in caring for patients who are bedwetters. You can call this foundation toll-free at 1-800-622-9010.

Relieve Your Child's Guilt

Once you have made an appointment with a doctor, you should start preparing for your child's visit. About three days before the visit (longer for an older child) discuss the bedwetting openly with your child, no matter how many times you may have done so before, and talk about the upcoming visit to the doctor. Because children generally feel a secret sense of guilt and shame about their bedwetting (even if they don't express it, and even if you have been very supportive and sympathetic), reassure your child again that the bedwetting is not her fault, that she did nothing to cause it, and that many children wet the bed. If you or your spouse were bedwetters as children, tell your child; knowing that this condition runs in the family and is not brought on by any misbehavior will relieve her of her guilt feelings more effectively than any other information. Be sure to explain that going to the doctor is not a punishment; the doctor's job is to try to find the cause and to find out how to cure the bedwetting.

Tell Your Child What to Expect at the Pediatrician's Office

Explain (at your child's level of understanding) that there are many different things in the body that can cause bedwetting, so the doctor will need information about the bedwetting and will need to examine many things. Let your child know that the doctor will examine many parts of his body, even his most private areas, which will make him feel a little squeamish, but that examining is what doctors must do to find what is causing the bedwetting.

In your explanation, use language that is simple and gentle. Make sure your child understands that what you have taught him about the need for privacy for the "private" parts of the body is still true, but that parents, doctors, and nurses sometimes need to examine children; those are the only exceptions. Reassure your child that he has a very nice doctor—and that you will be in the room with him the whole time. (However, an older child may prefer to be accompanied in the examining room by the same-sex parent or no parent at all, and that choice should be respected.)

Encourage your child to ask questions, and then answer them as truthfully as possible without going into alarming detail. Children of any age can "get a handle on things" and cope much better if they know in advance what is going to happen and why it is necessary. They also benefit from knowing that many other children have the same problem and have been through the same thing, so be sure to mention this. Over a period of days, additional questions may surface that will give you some insight into your child's fears and misconceptions. Be sincere in allaying fears and correcting misconceptions.

Be honest. Let your child know that the pediatrician or family doctor may need the help of other doctors to discover the cause of the bedwetting, and that your child may be asked to visit another doctor (specialist) to take X-ray pictures or to discover allergies, or an illness, or something that needs fixing in the part of the body that makes urine.

Tell Your Child What to Expect at the Specialist's Office

If a visit to a specialist is required—such as a specialist in urology, allergies, or endocrinology—prepare your child by using steps similar to those you used for the earlier visit to the primary-care physician: Discuss the bedwetting; dispel guilt and fears; correct misconceptions; share information about what to expect in the examination; and encourage questions.

Vicki L. Squires, director of Child Life Services at a Texas hospital, writes that unfamiliarity and unpredictability contribute to feelings of vulnerability in children. You yourself may know very little about the specialist's examination or what to anticipate at the specialist's office. Therefore, when you are making the appointment to see the specialist, ask the receptionist, office nurse, or doctor to tell you about the sequence of events that will occur in the visit so you can prepare your child for them. (During the same telephone call, also ask about special preparations, such as the need to bring a urine sample from home or the need to withhold food and/or water, etc.)

If your child needs to be examined by a urologist and you are seeking one who avoids the procedures I advised against in chapter 9, this is an opportune time to ask about the procedures and to accept or reject the urologist, based on her procedures.

If you make the appointment, tell your child gently but honestly what she can expect at the specialist's office. Let her know (in neutral, nonalarming words) that there may be some embarrassing, uncomfortable, or even painful tests or procedures (such as the ones described in chapter 9 for urological examinations). Let her know that the doctor will need to "drum on her tummy," "see if the opening of her 'pee-pee' [or whatever word you use with your child] is big enough," and "check for problems where 'number two' comes out." If a catheter needs to be inserted for a conscious voiding cystourethrogram (since most physicians do not use my unconscious method), explain that the doctor may ask an "X-ray specialist to put in a very, very thin tube and put a special liquid into it that will show on X-ray pictures the shape of the things inside her body that make urine." This will "sting a little for only half a minute while it is going in."

If the specialist needs to take a little blood for testing, your child may become secretly fearful that "taking blood" means taking all her blood. Explain that the body contains a lot of blood and that only a very little bit of it is taken for testing.

Explain that some children think that the procedures are punishment for bedwetting, but those children are very much mistaken: The doctor needs to examine and use tests to find the cause of the bedwetting and to try to cure it.

Gather Important Information for the Physician

One of the most important things you must do in preparation for your child's visit to the doctor is to gather necessary information. This is true whether the visit is to the family doctor, the pediatrician, or the specialist. Each doctor needs similar information to make an informed diagnosis.

It's very easy to become "rattled" at the doctor's office when you are trying to remember the details of your child's or the family's medical history or the symptoms you've been noticing in your child for some time. Yet these items of information are crucial for arriving at a correct diagnosis. The thing to do is to sit down a few days before the doctor visit and make two lists, which you can call "Family Medical History" and "My Child's Medical History and Symptoms." Where necessary, refer to medical records you have stored away and make informational calls to your parents and in-laws.

Complete a Family Medical-History List

The family medical-history list should contain answers to the following questions:

• Did you, your spouse, or any close members of your families (brothers, sisters, parents, uncles, aunts, grandparents) ever have kidney disease? Any form of urinary tract disorder? Bowel problems?

• Did you, your spouse, or immediate family members wet the bed in childhood?

• Do you or your spouse currently have any daytime or nighttime urinary symptoms?

• Are there other children in the family who wet?

• Did you, your spouse, or any close members of your families ever have diabetes? (If so, what type of diabetes? At what age did it start?) Allergies? Sickle-cell anemia? Thyroid disease? Attention deficit disorder?

List Your Child's Medical History and Symptoms

The list of your child's history and symptoms should include information about any experience your child may be having now, or any he may have had in the past, with the following (include approximate date or age, and details):

• Inflammation of the kidneys (nephritis)?
• Urinary infection?
• Diabetes? (Type?)
• Sickle-cell anemia?
• Thyroid disease?
• Allergies? Food intolerances?
• Pinworms?
• Constipation or encopresis (more than occasional)?
• Inflammation of the genital or anal area?
• Hemorrhoids?
• Pain or tenderness in the abdomen or the back?
• Pain during urination or bowel movement?
• Excessive thirst?
• Frequent tiredness?
• Problems with tonsils, adenoids, nasal congestion, mouth breathing, snoring (that could point to sleep apnea)?
• Sleepwalking, sleeptalking, nightmares, night terrors?
• Excessively heavy sleep?

In addition, list all other past and present diseases and conditions, injuries, surgeries, and hospitalizations, along with the approximate date (or age of your child) for each. Include any other symptoms or unusual things you may have noticed about your child, no matter how unrelated they may seem to bedwetting.

The list should also answer the following questions:

- Has my child been bedwetting since birth (primary wetting), or did he have a period of dryness (about six months or longer) before his present bedwetting (secondary wetting)?
- Does my child have daytime urinary symptoms: Frequent urination (enough to be troublesome in the classroom or on trips)? Urgency (rushing to the bathroom)? Spotting or wetting underclothes? Clutching the genital area? Jigging up and down? Rocking on the heel [for a girl]? Squeezing the thighs together?
- How many times a night does bedwetting occur? How many times a week?
- On dry nights, does my child get up one or more times to go to the bathroom?
- Do his underpants become stained with stool?
- Does he generally drink a great deal of water during the day?
- Does he snore during the night?
- If wetting started after about six months or more of dryness, was it preceded by a very stressful event such as the start of school? Birth of a new baby? Hospitalization? Divorce or death in the family? Separation from home and/or family?

The reason you should start this list at least several days before the doctor visit is that you have to make observations to answer questions such as these:

- How many times does my child urinate during the day?
- How much does he void each time? (Use an ordinary measuring cup.) Does the urine have definite color, or is it almost colorless?
- [For a boy] Does the urinary stream come out with good force, or does it dribble out? Does it spray, start, and stop? Does it splatter the floor or the toilet bowl? Does it form an oval with a thin center as it exits, or does it form a narrow, straight stream?
- [For a girl] Is there irritation or inflammation in the vulval area? Does she say she has pain, discomfort, itching, or burning in this area?
- Does my child have irritation or inflammation in the anal area?

If the doctor fails to ask you about any of these items, mention them anyway. Make a photocopy of your list, and leave it with the doctor. Keep a copy for your own records and another for use with other doctors.

PREPARING FOR THE HOSPITAL AND SURGERY

Things Are Different Today

Like many parents, you may have heard an older generation's stories of terrible childhood experiences in a hospital—or you may have endured a bad experience yourself. Now you may be afraid that your child will suffer similarly. Take heart!

The conditions that fostered those bad experiences no longer exist in most North American hospitals. First, many of the surgical procedures that used to keep a child in the hospital several or many overnights are now "same day" procedures with no overnights, except in very difficult or complicated cases. For example, the urological procedures described in the previous chapter are almost always same-day procedures. The child arrives in the morning, undergoes testing and/or surgery, and remains in the hospital for about three or four additional hours. Then he returns to his own bed, in his own home, the same day.

Second, most U.S. hospitals and at least half of all Canadian hospitals today permit you to remain with your child at all times except during the surgery. You can accompany your child to the operating room, stay with her during the induction of anesthesia, and be escorted back to the recovery room when she begins waking up. Your child will not even know that you were away from her side.

Even if your child is in the hospital for a rare problem that requires hospitalization for more than a day, almost all hospitals will now permit you to stay with your child around the clock. (They will provide you with a folding bed beside your child's bed.) And they will welcome your participation in many aspects of your child's care. Your child will not be confined to bed, but will play with other noncontagious children and with toys, games, and crafts in the playrooms as soon as he is able. (Even children who are receiving intravenous fluids are provided with portable, rolling supports for their IV bags, which they can take with them wherever they go.) Hospitals now recognize that these measures speed recovery.

Modern accommodation of your child's needs and yours is vastly different from the lack of accommodation in your grandparents' and parents' youth—when hospital stays were long, children were confined to their beds, and parents were forbidden to stay with their children or even visit them more than once a week for two hours. It is also different from the time of your own youth, when many hospitals did not permit parents to accompany children through the induction of the anesthesia nor to remain in the hospital with them overnight.

Third, in recent years enormous improvements have been made in anesthesia and the way it is given and monitored. Today anesthesia is very safe; monitoring is assisted by state-of-the-art technology; and anesthesiologists are trained to work with children. (You will learn more about the safety of anesthesia later in this chapter.)

Finally, almost all hospitals today have specially trained nurses or child-life specialists who conduct excellent orientation programs and preoperative hospital tours for both children and parents before the day of the surgery. You and your child should certainly take advantage of the hospital's orientation program and tour—which you can think of as a "familiarization" session—to alleviate fear and anxiety. (You will find a more complete description of hospital orientation programs later in this chapter.)

Choose a Hospital, Specialist, and Anesthetist

You probably know that the hospital and specialist come in a kind of "package." The specialist is affiliated with a particular hospital, or has operating privileges in one hospital or a very few hospitals. Therefore, if your pediatrician requests that your child be seen by a specialist, and if there is any chance that the specialist may have to test or treat your child in a hospital, you may want to choose the hospital first.

The New York Times health writer Jane Brody, writing about stays longer than same-day, suggested (as do many other sources) that parents select a hospital that permits or arranges for the following:

- A parent accompanying the child to the operating room and during the induction of anesthesia, until it takes effect.
- Overnight stays by a parent in the child's room.

- Unlimited visiting hours for parents and siblings.
- Parents' participation in the care of the child (including massages, baths, feeding, and play).
- Respectful, forthright responses to parents' questions and concerns (without an adversarial tone).
- A prehospitalization tour and education program.

If your child's procedure involves only a same-day stay, you still want to make sure that the hospital you select addresses your concerns with respect, offers a well-designed orientation session before the day of surgery, and enables you to stay with your child for the entire time except the operating period.

Once you have decided on the best hospital, you can ask your child's pediatrician to recommend a specialist who has privileges in that hospital. For example, if you are looking for a urologist, ask the pediatrician to recommend one who will avoid the tests I have warned against in chapter 9 and who has considerable experience and interest in working with children who bedwet. (Not all urologists have this experience or interest.) Get as much information as you can.

You can also call the appropriate department of the hospital you selected and ask for information and recommendations. Ask the same questions you asked your pediatrician. If the person you reach can't help you, ask to speak to the department chief. Don't be afraid to be persistent. Also, don't be afraid to ask whether recommended doctors have *current privileges* in that hospital.

Of course, you may prefer to tackle this process in reverse: You may want to find the most appropriate specialist first, and then look into the hospital or hospitals in which the specialist has privileges. Either way, you should look into both the specialist and hospital—and be satisfied initially with both—before you make the appointment for your child's examination.

Ultimately, you will receive the names of several specialists. If you have any doubts, consider contacting the medical board or the board of medical examiners (governmental agency) of the state in which these specialists practice. Ask the board for the most current information on the status of the physicians' licenses. This will not assure you of finding the best doctor, but it may help you avoid a doctor whose license is under probation, suspension, or revocation. (In every state, a surprising number of physicians continue to practice—some legally—despite disciplinary actions against them by medical boards. However, the medical board knows the status of each physician's license.)

At last you select a specialist, and you appear with your child for the examination at the office on the appointed day. You have copies of your lists of medical histories and symptoms. It's best that you have asked beforehand, but if you haven't, you must remember to ask about the examination procedures that this physician expects to use, and why she plans to use them. If the specialist is a urologist, you can discuss the examination procedures you learned about in chapter 9 of this book (take the book with you). A flexible physician will address your concerns and make accommodations. If the physician is going to conduct an undesirable test (such as the impractical "urodynamic" test to measure bladder pressure) despite your disapproval, you can refuse it. It would be better to find another urologist.

It is extremely important to have a specialist in whom you are confident. Let's suppose you have found that specialist, and after examining your child and consulting with you, he has scheduled your child for tests and/or surgery in the hospital. While you are still in the office, you need to ask to be scheduled also for the hospital's orientation program for children and parents. The hospital considers this to be the appropriate time and place to initiate this scheduling. If you wait, the orientation sessions may be fully booked on the day or days when you are available—or worse, all the spaces may be filled through the date of your child's admission. (Remember that in most hospitals, you and your child will not be permitted to participate in an orientation session on the day of the surgical procedure. You must do it before that day, preferably several days beforehand.)

This is also a good time to ask the specialist's or the office nurse's opinion on which anesthesiologist at the prospective hospital might have the best rapport with a child of your child's age and personality, and whether this anesthesiologist can be requested. Anesthesiologists are all different, even those who customarily work with children. The chemistry has to be very good. Perhaps the specialist can be of some assistance in arranging for the most suitable one. (Anyway, it can't hurt to ask.)

Prepare Your Child for the Hospital Experience

After the hospital date has been set, you should begin gathering appropriate books (and perhaps a videotape) from the hospital, library, bookstore, or helpful organizations. (See Appendix A for information about the Association for the Care of Children's Health and for lists of helpful books and videos.) Informative, sensitively written books about what to expect at the hospital are available for all age levels—toddlers, schoolchildren, teens, and parents. If your child is young, you can also buy him a toy "doctor's kit," which he can use to attend to a stuffed animal or a doll of his choice. (Don't suggest his favorite one; that might provoke anxiety.) Set all these things aside until a few days before your child's orientation session at the hospital (or a week before the session if your child is older). Give yourself enough time in preparing your child for the hospital because explanations will generate new questions.

Read one of the books with your child each day (preferably much earlier than bedtime) and discuss things as you go along. If your child is an adolescent, give him books appropriate for his age. Ask, during the reading and afterward, if he has any questions. If you don't know the answer to a question, tell him you don't know but will ask the doctor or a nurse, and you will tell him later. This lets him know that you are not avoiding the question in order to hide something frightening from him.

Discuss the approaching hospital experience. Once again, discuss the bedwetting and relieve your child of unspoken guilt feelings about it. Child psychiatrist John E. Meeks advises us (in *Hospital Medicine*) that younger children view all of the misfortunes that befall them as the results of their own actions. To illustrate, he describes a study of children who were *born with* orthopedic handicaps. When asked what had caused their disability, the vast majority of these children blamed it on their own disobedience of their parents' rules.

Working with somewhat older, hospitalized urology patients, pediatric psychiatrist Leah Beck and colleagues found that schoolchildren, some of them 10 years or older, believed that their illnesses and hospitalizations were punishments for being "bad."

With that in mind, it is important for you to explain the situation to your child in terms he can't easily misconstrue: "The doctors have found something that might be causing the bedwetting and they are going to try to fix it at the hospital. They think this may stop the bedwetting. None of this was caused by anything you did or said or thought."

Meeks, as well as Squires (and many others), also note that the greatest fear of children under age 6 is that they may be abandoned by their parent (or other principal nurturer). Assure your child that you or her other parent will be right beside her in the hospital all the time. And she may also take her favorite toy or stuffed animal with her.

Meeks and Squires say that (with respect to health care) pain, mutilation, needles (shots), and the knife are the next most common fears of children, especially children ages 6 through 12. Anesthesiologist Aaron L. Zuckerberg points out that this is especially true of boys whose surgery involves the penis.

So if your child asks, "Will it hurt?", address his fears. Assure him that the doctor will give him a special medicine called "anesthesia," which will make him sleep very deeply during the operation and keep him from feeling any pain. Be truthful: Tell him he may feel a little pain after the operation but that he can ask for medicine that will stop the pain, and a doctor or nurse will give it to him. Reassure him that all of his parts will be there when he wakes up, and the only difference will be that they will work better than they did before.

Use very nonthreatening words to describe things. For example, don't say that the doctor will "cut" you, or "open you up," or "make a hole." Say that the doctor will "make a small opening" or will "fix something that needs to be fixed." Also don't say that the anesthesiologist will "put you to sleep" or will "give you gas." Your child may have heard that a pet was "put to sleep" and never came back, and he may confuse gas with gasoline or with dangerous gas from the kitchen stove. Again, say that a doctor will "give you the special medicine that will make you sleep very deeply until the operation is finished, and then you will wake up."

According to Meeks, as well as to anesthesiologist Terry McGraw, the adolescent's fears of the hospital and surgery are very different from the younger child's. The adolescent is afraid of losing control, becoming dependent, "losing face," "losing her cool" (such as expressing feelings of fear, anxiety, or pain), and "sounding childish." The thing she fears the most at the hospital is the anesthesia; she worries about waking up during the operation, not waking up afterward, and dying.

Thus you need to assure your adolescent that she will not wake up during the operation; she will certainly wake up when the anesthesia is no longer being administered; and that, because anesthesia is very safe today, she won't die from it. The more information she receives about it, the better she can cope. Encourage her to read about it, to inform you about it from her reading, and to explain it to the family. Meeks says that intellectualization—or, in this case, "talking an anxiety to death"—is a coping defense appropriate to this age group.

Finally, be sure to attend your hospital's orientation program and preoperative tour with your child. If your child is young, tell him the day before the scheduled orientation session that both you and he will go to look at the hospital and play there, so he can see what it is like. If your child is older, discuss the orientation program, and let him know that it is a good place to ask and receive answers to any questions he has in mind.

Attend the Hospital Orientation Program and Tour

Orientation programs differ in detail, but they are generally similar. The following ones are fairly representative.

For young children, a daytime orientation in the hospital is conducted by a specially trained nurse or child-life specialist, usually for only one or two families at a time. The session begins in the family waiting room, where a 2-foot teddy bear or a large doll is a "patient." The child-life specialist "tells a story" about Teddy's surgery, which is going to take place "today." During the story, she encourages the children to help prepare Teddy as she introduces items slowly, telling about them in the simplest terms. The children help to put a name band and pajamas on Teddy. They make up a bed, "listen" with a stethoscope, take Teddy's temperature with a thermometer, and put a blood pressure cuff on him. They also put EKG patches and an anesthesia mask on him. Throughout, they are encouraged to ask questions, and they have their questions answered.

After this play therapy, the children and parents see a special orientation video and are encouraged to ask additional questions. Then they proceed to a tour of a real operating room, where the nurse introduces them to real anesthesia paraphernalia and other operating room equipment, and they can also become familiar with medical personnel dressed in "scrubs" and operating room clothing.

Then, while the children go on to explore the recovery room (sometimes called the *postanesthesia care unit*—PACU), a staff member briefs the parents about the anesthesia and how it will be administered to their child. Among other things, they explain that the psychological trauma that used to be caused by the induction of anesthesia is avoided today by using modern measures: familiarizing the child with the process beforehand; using anesthesiologists with expertise in working with children; and, extremely important, permitting the parent to remain with the child (sometimes holding the child on the parent's lap) during the induction.

For older children and their parents, the orientation program may take place in the daytime or the evening, for up to five families at a session. The nurse tells the story in an actual operating room, using the children instead of the teddy bear. The children handle real (but inoperative) equipment. Questions are encouraged and answered.

After the orientation session, the staff gives written instructions to the parents.

Once you and your child have attended the orientation program and tour, the hospital will no longer be an unknown, mysterious, or frightening idea to your child. It will be a familiar and interesting place, with friendly people. And both you and your child will be much better prepared.

Address Your Fears About Anesthesia

Many parents are deeply fearful for the safety of their children who are about to undergo anesthesia. They fear that their children may suffer physical effects or may die. Years ago these fears were justified. Today there is very little to fear.

Anesthesia is considered by experts to be remarkably safe. Researcher Marsha Cohen and two of her colleagues followed up on more than a hundred thousand patients of all ages who received anesthesia at a major Winnipeg (Canada) hospital between 1975 and 1984. They found that anesthesia doesn't add risk above such risks as the surgery itself, old age, and poor physical and medical condition of the patient. And, according to the *The New York Times*, a British study published in 1988 found that the death rate due to anesthesia was 1 in 185,000.

According to the experts, the chances of dying in a car accident on the way to the hospital are much greater than dying of anesthesia.

In recent years, anesthesia has come a long way. In an article published in *The Clinical Forum for Nurse Anesthetists*, anesthesiologist William Clayton Petty traced the evolution of safety in anesthesia, including the development and use of safer anesthetic gas, use of the microprocessor in the development of vastly improved monitoring technology (such as present-day automatic indirect blood pressure monitors, oximeters that photoelectrically measure the amount of oxygen in the blood, and capnography equipment that constantly measures the amount of carbon dioxide in the expired air), and the development of much more effective standards and laws to govern the practice of anesthesiology.

In 1985, for example, the American Society of Anesthesiologists (ASA) and the American Association of Nurse Anesthetists (AANA) adopted standards of basic monitoring; and in the same year, the ASA established the Anesthesia Patient Safety Foundation. In 1986, the Food and Drug Administration (FDA) released its *Anesthesia Apparatus Checkout Recommendations*, which were then endorsed by the ASA and the AANA. The introduction of monitoring of patients and monitoring of machines, as well as the change in anesthetic practice, have all contributed to anesthesia's present high level of safety.

Despite these reassurances, there are no guarantees. No drug or procedure is absolutely safe in 100 percent of patients. The chances that one's child will die of anesthesia are very remote, but other types of complications are also possible. An anesthesia-related problem can occur during the induction, operation, or recovery.

G. Edward Morgan Jr. and Maged S. Mikhail say in their book *Clinical Anesthesiology* that it is important for children to be free of colds and other viral respiratory infections for at least two to four weeks before general anesthesia. (If your child has had a viral upper respiratory infection within four weeks of the hospital date, tell the surgeon. He may want to postpone the procedure in the interests of safety.) Allergic upper respiratory conditions, on the other hand, can be coped with. Let the anesthesiologist know.

In one complication of anesthesia, according to Morgan and Mikhail (and other experts), some children experience a spasm of the laryngeal muscle (closure of the larynx, obstructing the flow of air to the lungs) during induction or toward the end of an anesthetic; however, the anesthesiologist can easily correct this problem.

A more serious but very rare complication of anesthesia (it occurs in only one out of fifteen thousand children) is an acute, overactive metabolic state in muscle tissue, which results in severe muscle rigidity and sometimes a high fever. This problem occurs after the induction of general anesthesia and, as described by Morgan and Mikhail, requires quick, complicated treatment—administered by a very experienced anesthesiologist along with additional staff.

Another rare complication affects children who have overactive thyroid glands; the problem involves those glands.

The most common problems related to anesthesia, however, are minor aftereffects. After awakening, some children become nauseous, and some have to vomit. The nausea generally subsides by itself, or the staff can give pediatric doses of antinausea medication. Sometimes a child awakens in the recovery room and begins to choke on secretions from the pharynx (mucous-membrane-lined passageway for air and food). The recovery room staff (sometimes aided by the parent) keeps such a child on his side so that secretions drain away from the area.

The material in this section has probably not answered all of your questions and concerns. Be sure to ask questions during the orientation (when your child is exploring the other room). If you need more answers, feel free to call the child-life specialist or even the anesthesiologist who is assigned to your child's surgery; ask any questions that may still be lingering in your mind.

SURGERY

The Day in the Hospital

On the morning of your child's scheduled surgery (which for purposes of this illustration will be same-day surgery), you will bring your child (holding her favorite toy) to the family waiting area of the hospital's same-day-surgery unit. She will have eaten no breakfast because anesthesia must be administered on an empty stomach. There will be toys and books in a corner of the waiting room.

You will probably be met by a nurse or child-life staff member. This person will assist you and your child, offer support, and help your child rehearse coping skills. Your child will be encouraged to play with the toys and books, but she may certainly sit on your lap and be cuddled if she prefers.

At the appropriate time, you (or your spouse) will be given special operating room garb, such as a gown, cap, etc., which you will wear to accompany your child. Then you will be escorted by the surgeon into the operating room. There you may sit beside your child or hold her in your lap give support and encouragement as the anesthesiologist prepares her for surgery. (As many experts—including those mentioned above—have reported, the presence of the parent is crucial in preventing the psychological trauma that used to occur when parents were excluded.)

You may want to remind the anesthesiologist of any nasal or other respiratory problems your child may have (such as allergies, asthma, back-drip, mouth breathing, or sleep apnea).

The anesthesiologist will engage your child in conversation. Your child will probably receive no premedication. For most same-day surgeries, anesthesiologists no longer need to premedicate children to calm them before administering anesthesia. The parent's presence is usually sufficient. (This is good news, because the premedication takes longer than the anesthesia to wear off. Also, fewer drugs are better for your child.)

If your child is young, the anesthesiologist may tell her a story, or engage her in a game while passing anesthetic gas over her face until she is asleep. If your child is older, the anesthesiologist may permit her to choose the method of induction: the mask or the intravenous needle. Although anesthetic gas, delivered by a face mask, is the method used most often, an older child may prefer to have intravenous anesthesia. (A special anesthetic cream, called EMLA cream, applied to the skin can make the intravenous needle painless. However, it must be applied an hour before the anesthetic, so if your child prefers this method, you should request it earlier.) If the mask is used, it will probably be a clear face mask (rather than the old, black ones), and your child will probably have a choice of scents (such as orange, mint, etc.) that can be applied inside the mask. If your child has attended the hospital orientation, she may be allowed to apply the mask herself.

When your child is asleep, you will be escorted back to the family waiting room. After the surgery, recovery-room personnel will care for your child until the anesthesia begins to wear off; then they will call for you (or your spouse) when your child begins to awaken.

Just as it is urgently important for a parent to accompany a child through anesthesia, it is equally important (as the researchers have reported) for a parent to be with the child when she begins to wake up. A parent's face is the one she needs to see first. In the recovery room, you will remain with your child, to comfort her and possibly to participate in her care, until the doctor judges she is able to leave. Then you will help her dress and take her home.

The Recuperation Period

Since most children's surgical procedures are performed on a same-day basis, most of the recuperation takes place at home.

As a parent, you need to take the period of recuperation and inactivity into consideration when you are planning to schedule surgery. If the problem can wait, you may want to schedule it during your child's summer vacation from school or during your vacation from work.

What can you expect during the period of recuperation? Let's suppose that your child underwent a urological procedure to remove a small obstruction in the urethra. When he comes home, you may see that he has to urinate frequently for a while. If the underlying problem has been corrected completely, he may have no discomfort to speak of, or he may have discomfort for a while when he urinates. This temporary postoperative discomfort can usually be alleviated with simple Pediatric Tylenol.

However, in the rare case where the obstruction or obstructions have not all been removed, there may be greater discomfort or pain. If your child experiences continued discomfort when he urinates so that he becomes reluctant to urinate, if he does a lot of jigging, and if these problems persist for five days or more, it is likely that the obstructions were not fully removed. Tell the urologist about the symptoms. If he suspects a urinary infection, he may prescribe an antibiotic. If that doesn't help, he must reinvestigate.

Let's return to the situation where recovery is proceeding normally. When your child arrives home, his activities must be fully restricted for the first week. He is not permitted to go to school, lift, strain, jump, run, or wrestle. At the end of the week, the urologist will examine him and make new decisions about his activities. If your child still has some discomfort or urinary frequency, or if his urine contains any blood cells, the urologist will restrict all activity until the symptoms go and/or the urine clears. These restrictions are seldom needed for more than three weeks.

Results

Within a month, your child's daytime symptoms of frequent and urgent urination should disappear. Within four months, the bedwetting should disappear. For your child, a great burden will be lifted from life. For the family, life will be smoother.

In some cases, the daytime symptoms will disappear, but the bedwetting will continue if the child is a very heavy sleeper. If you find this to be true in your child's case, be sure to try the wetness alarm or vibration system described in chapter 3. Although it may not have worked before the surgical correction of the underlying abnormalities, it will probably resolve the wetting now.

NOTE TO THE READER

In farewell, I hope that this book has helped you, the parent, to understand the many causes of bedwetting, to strengthen your support of your child who bedwets, to navigate well in the health care system, and to discover the cure for your child's bedwetting. Best wishes!

APPENDIX A

BOOKS AND VIDEOS THAT CAN HELP YOU PREPARE YOUR CHILD FOR DOCTOR VISITS AND THE HOSPITAL

PUBLICATIONS AND VIDEOS OF THE ACCH

For the past three decades the Association for the Care of Children's Health (ACCH) has been the moving force behind the humanization of children's care in hospitals. We can thank the ACCH for such current hospital practices as orientation programs and tours conducted by certified child-life professionals; parents accompanying their children during induction of anesthesia, in the recovery room, overnight, and throughout the hospital stay; and expanded visiting hours for other family members. The ACCH also produces helpful, up-to-date books, booklets, and videos about children's health problems and health care. You may be especially interested in obtaining the following titles:

For Children: Visiting the Hospital, 1996 (20 pages).
For Teenagers: Visiting the Hospital, 1996 (20 pages).
Going to the Hospital, 1986 (20 pages).
A Pediatric Bill of Rights, 1991 (12 pages).
The Moon Balloon, by Joan Drescher. A book to help children express their feelings honestly and openly (36 pages).
For Parents and Caregivers: Your Child in the Hospital, 1996 (20 pages).
Clearing the Air: A Parent's Guide to the Operating Room (video: Nickel's Worth Productions).

Send your request to the association at 7910 Woodmont Avenue, Suite

300, Bethesda, MD 20814. Or call this helpful organization, toll-free, at 800-808-2224, for more information.

BOOKS AND VIDEOS FROM
BOOKSTORES AND LIBRARIES

The Berenstain Bears Go to the Doctor, by Stan and Jan Berenstain. New York: Random House, 1981 (preschool through grade 1).

Going to the Doctor, by Fred Rogers (of *Mr. Rogers' Neighborhood*). New York: G. P. Putnam's Sons, 1988 (preschool through grade 1).

Going to the Doctor, by T. Berry Brazelton. Reading, Mass.: Addison-Wesley, 1996 (elementary school).

Curious George Goes to the Hospital, by Margret and H. A. Rey. Boston: Houghton-Mifflin, 1966 (preschool through kindergarten).

Going to the Hospital, by Anne Civardi and Stephen Cartwright. Tulsa, Okla.: EDC Publishing, 1986 (preschool through grade 2).

Going to the Hospital, by Fred Rogers (of *Mr. Rogers' Neighborhood*). New York: G. P. Putnam's Sons, 1988 (preschool through grade 3).

A Visit to the Sesame Street Hospital (with Jim Henson's Muppets), by Deborah Hautzig. New York: Random House/Children's Television Workshop, 1985 (preschool through grade 3).

Why Am I Going to the Hospital?, by Claire Ciliotta and Carole Livingston. New York: Lyle Stuart, 1992 (grade 1 through grade 4).

The Hospital Book, by James Howe. New York: Morrow Junior Books, 1994 (grades 3 through 6).

Things to Know Before You Go to the Hospital, by Lisa Ann Marsoli. Morristown, N.J.: Silver Burdett, 1984 (grades 3 through 6).

Coping with a Hospital Stay, by Sharon Carter and Judy Monnig. New York: Rosen Publishing Group, 1987 (junior and senior high school).

Sesame Street Home Video Visits the Hospital (video). New York: Children's Television Workshop, 1990.

Mickey Visits the Hospital (filmstrip). Disney Educational Productions, 1988.

APPENDIX B
BIBLIOGRAPHY

Abe, K., et al. "Twin Study on Night Terrors, Fears, and Some Physiological and Behavioural Characteristics in Childhood." *Psychiatric Genetics*, vol. 3, no. 1, pp. 39–43, 1993.

Aberle, B., and P. Krepler. "Significance of Uroflometry in Children." *Urologe*, vol. 18, no. 5, pp. 289–295, September–October 1969.

Adams, Samuel S. "Incontinence of Urine in Children." *American Journal of Obstetrics*, vol. 17, pp. 657–671, 1884.

American Journal of Health-System Pharmacy. "Frequency of Sickle Cell Crises Cut by Hydroxyurea Use." AJHSP, vol. 52, no. 8, p. 778, April 15, 1995.

Anders, Thomas F., and Ellen D. Freeman. "Enuresis" (Chapter 28). In Joseph D. Noshpitz, ed., *Basic Handbook of Child Psychiatry*, vol. 2. New York: Basic Books, 1979.

Anonymous. "DDAVP Information Sheet and Prescribing Information." Rorer Pharmaceutical Corp., 1995.

Anonymous. *PACTS: Parents Assisting Children to Sleep* (booklet and brochure). Morristown, N.J.: Morristown Memorial Hospital, n.d.

Anonymous. *Shaping the Future of Children's Health Care.* Bethesda, Md.: Association for the Care of Children's Health, 1990.

Arena, M. G., et al. "Enuresis Risoria: Evaluation and Management." *Functional Neurology*, vol. 2, no. 4, pp. 579–582, October–December 1987.

Arnold, J. H. "Cystometry and Enuresis." *Journal of Urology*, vol. 96, p. 194, 1966.

Arnold, Samuel J. "Consequence of Childhood Urethral Disease." *Postgraduate Medicine*, vol. 43, pp. 193–198, March 1968.

Arnold, Samuel J. "Detrusor Instability in Primary Enuresis" (letter). *Urology*, vol. 42, no. 2, pp. 225–226, August 1993.

Arnold, Samuel J. "Disturbed Urinary Flow: Urethral Dynamics" (letter). *Journal of the American Medical Association*, vol. 204, no. 4, pp. 128–129, July 24, 1967.

Arnold, Samuel J. "Enuresis." *American Journal of Diseases of Children*, vol. 123, no. 1, p. 84, January 1972.

Arnold, Samuel J. "Enuresis" (letter). *Urology*, vol. 1, no. 3, p. 270, March 1973.

Arnold, Samuel J. "Enuresis, a Reappraisal." *Medical Tribune*, July 26, 1970.

Arnold, Samuel J. "Enuresis: Treatment with Imipramine" (letter). *Journal of the American Medical Association*, vol. 228, no. 3, pp. 289–290, April 15, 1974.

Arnold, Samuel J. "Genitourinary Disease Rate with Enuresis Noted" (Medical News). *Journal of the American Medical Association*, vol. 193, p. 354, 1965.

Arnold, Samuel J. "His and Hers" (letter). *New York Times Magazine*, p. 91, March 9, 1975.

Arnold, Samuel J. "Organic Causes Underlie Childhood Bedwetting" (Medical News). *Journal of the American Medical Association*, vol. 209, p. 193, 1969.

Arnold, Samuel J. "Problems in Treatment of Enuresis" (letter). *Journal of the American Medical Association*, vol. 194, no. 11, p. 200, December 12, 1965.

Arnold, Samuel J. "Stenotic Meatus in Children: An Analysis of 160 Cases." *Journal of Urology*, vol. 91, no. 4, pp. 357–360, April 1964.

Arnold, Samuel J. "Unrecognized Congenital Posterior Urethral 'Minivalves' in Men." *Urology*, vol. 41, no. 6, pp. 554–556, June 1993.

Arnold, Samuel J., and Roger Berg. "Conscious Dynamic Versus Unconscious Static Cystourethrography." *Journal of Urology*, vol. 118, no. 6, pp. 1030–1034, December 1977.

Arnold, Samuel J., and Arthur Ginsburg. "Charged Gold Leaf in Urology: 1. Urethral Meatotomy." *Journal of Urology*, vol. 96, no. 6, pp. 925–927, December 1966.

Arnold, Samuel J., and Arthur Ginsburg. "Enuresis" (letter). *Mayo Clinic Proceedings*, vol. 55, no. 9, pp. 586–587, September 1980.

Arnold, Samuel J., and Arthur Ginsburg. "Enuresis: Incidence and Pertinence of Genitourinary Disease in Healthy Enuretic Children." *Urology*, vol. 2, no. 4, pp. 437–443, October 1973.

Arnold, Samuel J., and Arthur Ginsburg. "Is Bedwetting Psychological?" (letter). *Lancet*, vol. 1, no. 8065, p. 658, March 25, 1978.

Arnold, Samuel J., and Arthur Ginsburg. "Pearls of Gold: Meatotomy, Circumcision, Urethrohymeneal Folds, Vasectomy, Peyronie's Disease" (letter). *Urology*, vol. 16, no. 6, pp. 661–662, December 1980.

Arnold, Samuel J., and Arthur Ginsburg. "Radiographic and Photoendoscopic Studies of Posterior Urethral Valves in Enuretic Boys." *Urology*, vol. 4, no. 2, pp. 145–154, August 1974.

Arnold, Samuel J., and Arthur Ginsburg. "Understanding and Managing Enuresis in Children." *Postgraduate Medicine*, vol. 58, no. 6, pp. 73–82, November 1975.

Arnold, Samuel J., and David L. Taylor. "Re: Urodynamic Studies in Enuresis and the Nonneurogenic Neurogenic Bladder" (letter). *Journal of Urology*, vol. 134, no. 1, p. 154, July 1985.

Arnold, Samuel J., et al. "Photo Studies of Urethral Varices. Hemorrhoids: A Forgotten Lesion." *Urology*, vol. 11, no. 1, pp. 19–27, January 1978.

Arnold, Samuel J, et al. "Prostatic Secretion and Urethral Flow: New Concepts and Preliminary Data." *Urology*, vol. 4, no. 4, pp. 67–72, October 1974.

Arnold, Samuel, et al. "Radiographic Criteria of Meatal and Distal Urethral Stenosis." *Urology*, vol. 1, no. 5, pp. 397–404, May 1973.

Avigne, Gail, and Tammy L. Phillips. "Pediatric Preoperative Tours." *AORN Journal*, vol. 53, no. 6, pp. 1458–1466, June 1991.

Bacopoulos, Christos, et al. "Primary Nocturnal Enuresis in Children with Vesicoureteral Reflux." *British Medical Journal, Clinical Research Edition*, vol. 294, no. 6573, pp. 678–679, 1987.

Bakwin, Harry, and Ruth M. Bakwin. *Clinical Management of Behavior Disorders in Children*, 2nd ed. Philadelphia: W. B. Saunders Co., 1960.

Bakwin, Henry. "Enuresis in Children." *Journal of Pediatrics*, vol. 58, no. 6, pp. 806–819, June 1961.

Bakwin, Henry. "Enuresis in Twins." *American Journal of Diseases of Children*, vol. 121, no. 3, pp. 222–225, March 1971.

Ballenger, Edgar D., et al. "Neglected Affections and Lesions of the Deep Urethra." *The American Journal of Surgery*, vol. 25, no. 2, pp. 201–210, August 1934.

Bamford, M. F. M., and G. Cruickshank. "Dangers of Intranasal Desmopressin for Nocturnal Enuresis" (letter). *Journal of the Royal College of General Practitioners*, pp. 345–346, August 1989.

Bass, Lee W. "Pollakiuria, Extraordinary Daytime Urinary Frequency: Experience in a Pediatric Practice." *Pediatrics*, vol. 87, no. 5, pp. 735–737, May 1991.

Beck, Leah, et al. "On a Children's Urology Service." *Social Work in Health Care*, vol. 4, no. 3, pp. 275–285, Spring 1979.

Best, Charles H., and Norman B. Taylor. *The Physiological Basis of Medical Practice*, 4th ed. Baltimore: The Williams and Wilkins Co., 1945.

Beuzard, Y. "Perspectives therapeutiques de la drepanocytose. [Therapeutic perspectives of Sickle-Cell Anemia.]" *Revue du Practicien*, vol. 42, no. 15, pp. 1908–1911, October 1992.

Bhatia, M., et al. "Attention Deficit Disorder with Hyperactivity Among Paediatric Outpatients." *Journal of Child Psychology and Psychiatry*, vol. 32, pp. 297–306, 1991.

Biederman, Joseph, et al. "Clinical Correlates of Enuresis in ADHD and Non-ADHD Children." *Journal of Child Psychology and Psychiatry*, vol. 36, no. 5, pp. 865–877, July 1995.

Biewald, W., and S. H. Duda. "Surgical Therapy of Congenital Urethral Stenosis in Girls by Meatoplasty." *International Urology and Nephrology*, vol. 19, no. 3, pp. 327–332, 1987.

Bigwood, Catherine. "The Environment Strikes Back." *Harper's Bazaar*, pp. 70–71, June 1972.

Birkasova, Marie, et al. "Desmopressin in the Management of Nocturnal Enuresis in Children: A Double-Blind Study." *Pediatrics*, vol. 62, no. 6, pp. 970–974, December 1978.

Bloom, David A. "The American Experience with Desmopressin." *Clinical Pediatrics*, Special Edition, pp. 28–31, 1993.

Braithwaite, J. Vernon. "The Child Who Wets the Bed." *General Practitioner*, vol. 3, no. 4, pp. 53–59, April 1951.

Bray, George W. "The Allergic Child." *British Journal of Children's Diseases*, vol. 29, no. 337, pp. 1–9, January, 1932.

Bray, George W. "Enuresis of Allergic Origin." *Archives of Diseases in Childhood*, vol. 6, pp. 251–253, 1931.

Bray, George W., *Recent Advances in Allergy*. London: J. and A. Churchill, 1931.

Brocklebank, J. T., and S. R. Meadow. "Cure of Giggle Micturition." *Archives of Diseases in Childhood*, vol. 56, no. 3, pp. 232–234, March 1981.

Brodny, M. Leopold, and Samuel A. Robins. "Enuresis: The Use of Cystourethrography in Diagnosis." *Journal of the American Medical Association*, vol. 126, pp. 1000–1006, December 16, 1944.

Brody, Jane E. "A Hospitalization Need Not Traumatize a Child." *The New York Times*, p. 71, September 22, 1982.

Brody, Jane E. "Personal Health: Silence on Fecal Incontinence Is Harmful." *The New York Times*, p. 72, January 29, 1992.

Broughton, Roger J. "Sleep Disorders: Disorders of Arousal?" *Science*, vol. 159, pp. 1070–1078, March 8, 1968.

Buck, P., and P. Sauvage. "Les Lesions Organiques de Infant Enuretique." *Journal of Medicine of Strassbourg*, vol. 4, nos. 9–10, pp. 643–648, 1973.

Burkhard, Carl E. "Manifestations of Hypersensitivity in the Genitourinary System." *Urologic and Cutaneous Review*, pp. 290–295, 1951.

Burrows, Edmund H. *Urethral Lesions in Infancy and Childhood Studied with Micturition Cystourethrography*. Springfield, Ill.: Charles C Thomas, 1973.

Campbell, Edward W., Jr., and John D. Young, Jr. "Enuresis and Its Relationship to Electroencephalographic Disturbances." *Journal of Urology*, vol. 96, no. 6, pp. 947–949, December 1966.

Campbell, Meredith F. "A Clinical Study of Persistent Enuresis." *New York State Journal of Medicine*, vol. 34, p. 190, 1934.

Campbell, Meredith F. "Enuresis." *Archives of Pediatrics*, vol. 54, no. 4, pp. 187–197, April 1937.

Campbell, Meredith F. "Enuresis." In Meredith F. Campbell, ed., *Principles of Urology*. Philadelphia: W. B. Saunders Co., 1957.

Campbell, Meredith F. "Enuresis: Its Urologic Aspects." *Journal of Urology*, vol. 28, no. 3, pp. 255–270, September 1932.

Carpenter, Richard O. "Disorders of Elimination" (Sec. 29.16). In Frank

A. Oski, et al., eds., *Principles and Practice of Pediatrics*, 2nd ed. Philadelphia: J. B. Lippincott Co., 1994.

Charache, S. "Pharmacological Modification of Hemoglobin F Expression in Sickle-Cell Anemia: An Update on Hydroxyurea Studies." *Experientia*, vol. 42, no. 9, pp. 126–132, February 15, 1993.

Check, William A. "How One Hospital Allays Children's Fears of Surgery." *JAMA*, vol. 242, no. 23, p. 2526, December 7, 1979.

Clark, R. Barkley. "Psychosocial Aspects of Pediatrics & Psychiatric Disorders." In William W. Hay, Jr., et al., eds., *Current Pediatric Diagnosis & Treatment*, 12th ed. Norwalk, Conn.: Appleton & Lange, 1995.

Cobb, Ben G., et al. "Congenital Stricture of the Proximal Urethral Bulb." *Journal of Urology*, vol. 99, no. 5, pp. 629–631, May 1968.

Code, C. F., et al. "Histamine in Human Disease." *Mayo Clinic Proceedings*, vol. 39, pp. 715–737, 1964.

Cohen, Marsha M., et al. "Does Anesthesia Contribute to Operative Mortality?" JAMA, vol. 260, no. 19, pp. 2859–2863, November 18, 1988.

Colodny, Arnold H. "Extraordinary Urinary Frequency" (letter). *Pediatrics*, vol. 87, no. 4, p. 582, April 1991. (With reply by J. Zoubek, et al.)

Cornil, Carl. *Urethral Obstruction in Boys: Diagnosis and Treatment of Congenital Valves of the Posterior Urethra.* New York: Excerpta Medica/ Amerkan Elsevier, 1975.

Crook, William G. "Food Allergy—The Great Masquerader." *Pediatric Clinics of North America*, vol. 22, no. 1, pp. 227–238, February 1975.

Crook, William G., et al. *Hidden Food Allergy: A Common and Often Unrecognized Cause of Chronic Symptoms in Children.* Jackson, Tenn.: The Children's Clinic, 1981. Also: Scientific Exhibit, 37th Annual Congress of American College of Allergists, Washington, D.C., April 5–7, 1981.

Cutler, Charles, et al. "Radiographic Findings in Children Surveyed for Enuresis." *Urology*, vol. 11, no. 5, pp. 480–482, May 1978.

Dalton, Richard. "Vegetative Disorders." In Waldo E. Nelson, ed., *Nelson Textbook of Pediatrics*, Part III, 1995. Philadelphia: W. B. Saunders, pp. 79–81.

De Backer, E., and D. L. Williams. "Cineradiology in Enuretic Girls: The Wide Bladder-Neck Syndrome." *British Journal of Urology*, vol. 33, p. 486, 1961.

Dimson, F. B. "Desmopressin as a Treatment for Enuresis" (letter). *Lancet*, no. 8024, p. 1260, June 11, 1977.

Dimson, F. B. "DDAVP and Urine Osmolality in Refractory Enuresis." *Archives of Disease in Childhood*," vol. 61, pp. 1104–1107, 1986.

Dische, Sylvia, et al. "Childhood Nocturnal Enuresis: Factors Associated with Outcome of Treatment with an Enuresis Alarm." *Developmental Medicine and Child Neurology (London)*, vol. 25, pp. 67–80, 1983.

Dittman, K. S., and K. A. Blinn. "Sleep Levels in Enuresis." *American Journal of Psychiatry*, vol. 12, pp. 913–920, 1955.

Djurhuus, Jens C., et al. "Monosymptomatic Bedwetting." *Scandinavian Journal of Urology & Nephrology* (Supplement), vol. 141, pp. 7–19, 1992.

Djurhuus, Jens C., et al., eds. *Nocturnal Enuresis: A New Strategy for Treatment Against a Physiological Background.* Karlshamn, Sweden: Lagerblads Tryckeri, 1992, pp. 3–29.

Dollinger, Stephen J. "Lightening Strike Disaster Among Children." *British Journal of Medical Psychology*, vol. 58, pp. 375–383, 1985.

Egger, J., et al. "Effect of Diet Treatment on Enuresis in Children with Migraine or Hyperkinetic Behavior." *Clinical Pediatrics*, vol. 31, no. 5, pp. 302–306, May 1992.

Eiberg, Hans, et al. "Assignment of Dominant Inherited Nocturnal Enuresis (ENUR1) to Chromosome 13." *Nature Genetics*, vol. 10, no. 3, pp. 354–356, July 1995.

Eisenstaedt, J. S. "Allergy and Drug Hypersensitivity of the Urinary Tract." *Journal of Urology*, vol. 65, no. 1, pp. 154–159, January 1951.

Esperanca, M., and John W. Gerard. "Nocturnal Enuresis: Comparison of the Effect of Imipramine and Dietary Restriction on Bladder Capacity." *Canadian Medical Association Journal*, vol. 101, pp. 65–68, December 13, 1969.

Evans, J. H. C., and S. R. Meadow. "Desmopressin for Bedwetting: Length of Treatment, Vasopressin Secretion, and Response." *Archives of Disease in Childhood*, vol. 67, pp. 184–188, 1992.

Feehan, M., et al. "A 6-Year Follow-up of Childhood Enuresis: Prevalence in Adolescence and Consequences for Mental Health." *Journal of Paediatrics and Child Health*, vol. 26, pp. 75–79, 1990.

Fergusson, David M., and L. John Horwood. "Nocturnal Enuresis and Behavioral Problems in Adolescence: A 15-Year Longitudinal Study." *Pediatrics*, vol. 94, no. 5, pp. 662–668, November 1994.

Fergusson, David M., et al. "Secondary Enuresis in a Birth Cohort of New Zealand Children." *Paediatric and Perinatal Epidemiology*, vol. 4, pp. 53–63, 1990.

Ferster, A., et al. "Bone Marrow Transplantation for Severe Sickle-Cell Anemia." *British Journal of Haematology*, vol. 80, no. 1, pp. 102–105, January 1992.

Figueroa, T. Ernesto, et al. "Enuresis in Sickle-Cell Disease." *Journal of Urology*, vol. 153, no. 6, pp. 1987–1989, June 1995.

Fisher, O. D., and Forsythe, W. I. "Micturating Cystourethrography in the Investigation of Enuresis." *Archives of Disease in Childhood*, vol. 29, pp. 460–471, 1954.

Fitzwater, Douglas, and Macknin, Michael. "Risk-Benefit Ratio in Enuresis Therapy" (editorial). *Clinical Pediatrics*, pp. 308–310, May 1992.

Fjellestad-Paulson A., et al. "Comparison of Intranasal and Oral Desmopressin for Nocturnal Enuresis." *Archives of Disease in Childhood*, vol. 62, pp. 674–677, 1987.

Frankin, John. *Molecules of the Mind: The Brave New Science of Molecular Psychology.* New York: Athenaeum, 1987.

Gastaut, Henri, and Roger J. Broughton. "A Clinical and Polygraphic Study of Episodic Phenomena During Sleep." In D. Wortis, ed., *Recent Advances in Biological Psychiatry*, Chapter 22. New York: Plenum Press, 1974, pp. 197–221.

Gershwin, M. Eric, and Edwin L. Klingelhofer. *Conquering Your Child's Allergies.* Reading, Mass.: Addison-Wesley Publishing Co., 1989.

Gill, Samuel E. "Nocturnal Enuresis, Experience with Evacuated Children." *The British Medical Journal*, August 10, 1940.

Goleman, Daniel. "A Genetic Clue to Bedwetting Is Located." *The New York Times*, p. 8, July 1, 1995.

Gonzales, Ricardo. "Urologic Disorders in Infants and Children." In Waldo E. Nelson, ed., *Nelson Textbook of Pediatrics*, 15th ed. Philadelphia: W. B. Saunders Co., 1996, p. 1531.

Goswami, R., et al. "Micturition Disturbances in Hyperthyroidism." *British Journal of Urology*, vol. 75, no. 5, pp. 678–679, May 1995.

Gudzhabidze, D. B., et al. "Morphological Changes in the Stenotic Distal Portion of the Urethra in Girls." *Urologiia I Nefrologiia (Mosk)*, vol. 3, pp. 64–69, May/June 1991.

Gupta, A. K., et al. "Daytime Urinary Frequency Syndrome in Childhood." *Indian Pediatrics*, vol. 27, pp. 752–754, July 1990.

Handford, Allen H., et al. "Sleep Disturbances and Disorders." In Melvin Lewis, ed., *Child and Adolescent Psychiatry: A Comprehensive Textbook.* Baltimore: Williams & Wilkins, 1991, chap. 62.

Hanner, Robert. "Enuresis and Food Sensitivity" (letter). *Australian Family Physician*, vol. 18, no. 2, p. 86, February 1989.

Harrow, Benedict, R. "The Rarity of Bladder-Neck Obstruction in Children." *Journal of Pediatrics*, vol. 69, no. 5, pp. 853–854, November 1966.

Harrow, Benedict R., et al. "A Critical Examination of Bladder-Neck Obstruction in Children." *Journal of Urology*, vol. 98, no. 5, pp. 613–617, 1967.

Harzmann, R., and R. Chiari. "Etiology and Therapy of Recurring Urinary Tract Infection and Enuresis in Girls." *Urologia Internationalis*, vol. 30, p. 455, 1975.

Haubensak, K., and A. Koch. "Urodynamic Studies Among Enuretics." *Urologia Internationalis*, vol. 31, nos. 1–2, pp. 87–92, 1976.

Hellman, Daniel S., and Nathan Blackman. "Enuresis, Firesetting, and Cruelty to Animals: A Triad Predictive of Adult Crime." *American Journal of Psychiatry*, vol. 122, pp. 1431–1434, June 1966.

Hendren, W. Hardy III. "Posterior Urethral Valves." In Keith W. Ashcroft, ed., *Pediatriatic Urology*, chap. 14. Philadelphia: W. B. Saunders Co., 1990.

Hendren, W. Hardy III. "Posterior Urethral Valves in Boys: A Broad Clinical Spectrum." *Journal of Urology*, vol. 106, no. 2, pp. 298–307, August 1971.

Hensle, Terry W. "Pediatric Urology Medal: W. Hardy Hendren III." *Journal of Urology*, vol. 152, p. 758, August 1994.

Hjalmas, Kelm. "SWEET, the Swedish Enuresis Trial." *Proceedings of the Second International Enuresis Research Center (IERC) Workshop: Pathophysiology and Treatment*, pp. 89–93, Aarhus, Denmark, May 27–29, 1995.

Hjalmas, Kelm, and Bengt Bengtsson. "Efficacy, Safety, and Dosing of

Desmopressin for Nocturnal Enuresis in Europe." *Clinical Pediatrics*, Special Edition, pp. 19–24, 1993.

Hogg, Ronald J., and Doug Husmann. "The Role of Family History in Predicting Response to Desmopressin in Nocturnal Enuresis." *Journal of Urology*, vol. 150, pp. 444–445, August 1993.

Holubar, J., et al. "Urethral Dilatation in the Treatment of Urinary Tract Infections in Girls." *Ceskoslovenska Pediatrie*, vol. 46, nos. 8–9, pp. 408–409, September 1991.

Horesh, Arthur J. "Allergy and Recurrent Urinary Tract Infections in Childhood–II." *Annals of Allergy*, vol. 36, pp. 174–179, March 1976.

Howard, H. H., et al. "Urodynamic Studies in Primary Nocturnal Enuresis." *China Medical Journal* (Taipei), vol. 41, p. 227, 1988.

Hradec, E., et al. "Significance of Urethral Obstruction in Girls." *Urologia Internationalis*, vol. 28, no. 6, pp. 440–452, 1973.

Hsu, Chen-Chin, and Yi-Sen Chiu. "An Epidemiological Study on Enuresis Among School Age Children: 2nd Report." A Study on the Reliability of Information Obtained Through Questionnaires Regarding the Presence and Absence of Enuresis." *Formosan Medical Association Journal*, vol. 68, p. 39, January 28, 1969.

Hunsballe, J. M., et al. "Polyuric and Non-Polyuric Bedwetting: Pathenogenic Differences in Nocturnal Enuresis." *Proceedings of the Second International Enuresis Research Center (IERC) Workshop: Pathophysiology and Treatment*, pp. 77–79, Aarhus, Denmark, May 27–29, 1995.

Husmann, Douglas A. "Enuresis." *Urology*, vol. 48, no. 2, pp. 184–193, 1996.

Jakobsson, I. "Unusual Presentation of Adverse Reactions to Cow's Milk Proteins." *Klinische Padiatrie*, vol. 197, no. 4, pp. 360–362, July–August 1985.

Jarvelin, Marjo R., et al. "Aetiological and Precipitating Factors for

Childhood Enuresis." *Acta Paediatrica Scandinavica*, vol. 80, no. 3, pp. 361–369, March 1991.

Jarvelin, Marjo R., et al. "Life Changes and Protective Capacities in Enuretic and Non-Enuretic Children." *Journal of Child Psychology and Psychiatry*, vol. 31, no. 5, pp. 763–774, July 1990.

Jarvelin, Marjo R., et al. "Screening of Urinary Tract Abnormalities Among Day- and Night-Wetting Children." *Scandinavian Journal of Urology and Nephrology*, vol. 24, no. 3, pp. 181–189, 1990.

Johnson, Edward L. "Evaluation of Dorsal Urethroplasty in Female Children." *Journal of Urology*, vol. 109, no. 1, pp. 113–114, January 1973.

Johnson, S. Harris III, and Matthew Marshall, Jr. "Enuresis." *Journal of Urology*, vol. 71, no. 5, pp. 554–559, May 1954.

Jones, Betty, et al. "Recurrent Urinary Infections in Girls: Relation to Enuresis." *Canadian Medical Association Journal*, vol. 106, no. 2, pp. 127–130, January 22, 1972.

Kales, Anthony, et al. "Sleep Disorders: Insomnia, Sleepwalking, Night Terrors, Nightmares, and Enuresis." *Annals of Internal Medicine*, vol. 106, no. 4, pp. 582–592, April 1987.

Kallio, Jaana, et al. "Severe Hyponatremia Caused by Intranasal Desmopressin for Nocturnal Enuresis." *Acta Paediatrica*, vol. 82, pp. 881–882, 1993.

Kane, Christopher J., et al. "Posterior Urethral Valves in Adults." *Infections in Urology*, pp. 111–115, July/August 1994.

Karlson, Stig. "Experimental Studies on the Functioning of the Female Urinary Bladder and Urethra." *Scandinavian Journal of Obstetrics and Gynecology*, vol. 33, pp. 285–307, 1953.

Key, David W., et al. "Low-Dose DDAVP in Nocturnal Enuresis." *Clinical Pediatrics*, pp. 299–301, May 1992.

Khanna, Om P., et al. "Histamine Receptors in Urethrovesical Smooth Muscle." *Urology*, vol. 10, no. 4, pp. 375–381, October 1977.

Kindall, L., and T. T. Nickels. "Allergy of the Pelvic Urinary Tract in the Female." *Journal of Urology*, vol. 61, pp. 222–227, 1949.

Kitagawa, K. "A Study of Functional Enuresis in Children: Voiding Cystourethrographic and Cystometric Study." *Nippon Hinyokika Gakkai Zasshi* (Japanese Journal of Urology), vol. 71, no. 7, pp. 664–680, July 1980.

Kjellberg, Sven R., et al. *The Lower Urinary Tract in Childhood.* Chicago: Year Book Medical Publishers, 1957.

Koerner, Celide Barnes, and Hugh A. Sampson. "Diets and Nutrition." In Dean D. Metcalf, Hugh A. Sampson, and Ronald A. Simon, eds., *Food Allergy: Adverse Reactions to Foods and Food Additives.* 2nd ed. Cambridge, Mass.: Blackwell Science, 1997, chap. 32.

Koff, S. A. "Why Is Desmopressin Sometimes Ineffective at Curing Bedwetting?" *Proceedings of the Second International Enuresis Research Center (IERC) Workshop: Pathophysiology and Treatment*, Aarhus, Denmark, May 27–29, 1995.

Kolvin, I. "Enuresis in Childhood." *Practitioner*, vol. 214, pp. 33–45, 1975.

Kolvin, I., et al., eds. *Bladder Control and Enuresis* (Clinics in Developmental Medicine, nos. 48/49). Philadelphia: J. B. Lippincott Co., 1973.

Kondo, Atsuo, et al. "Functional Obstruction of the Female Urethra: Relevance to Refractory Bedwetting and Recurrent Urinary Tract Infection." *Neurology and Urodynamics*, vol. 13, no. 5, pp. 541–546, 1994.

Kondo, Atsuo, et al. "Holding Postures Characteristic of Unstable Bladder." *Journal of Urology*, vol. 134, no. 4, pp. 702–704, October 1985.

Kozeny, G. A., and W. S. Wood. "Secondary Enuresis Associated with Hyperthyroidism." *Journal of Family Practice*, vol. 23, no. 3, pp. 273–274, September 1986.

Kroll, K. "Curing Nocturnal Enuresis: A Simple Program That Works." *Urology Digest*, pp. 13–15, October 1975.

Landon, Michael. Interview in *Family Weekly*, August 17, 1975.

Langlois, P. J. "Treatment of Bedwetting." *Journal of the American Medical Association*, vol. 234, p. 1116, 1975.

Lennert, J. B., and J. J. Mowad. "Enuresis: Evaluation of Perplexing Symptoms." *Urology*, vol. 13, no. 2, pp. 27–29, January 1979.

Levine, Melvin D. "The Schoolchild with Encopresis." *Pediatrics in Review*, vol. 2, no. 9, pp. 285–287, March 1981.

Linderholm, B. E. "The Cystometric Findings in Enuresis." *Journal of Urology*, vol. 96, p. 718, 1966.

Littleton, R. H., et al. "Eosinophilic Cystitis: An Uncommon Form of Cystitis." *Journal of Urology*, vol. 127, no. 1, pp. 132–133, January 1982.

Lizasoain, Olga, and Aquilino Polaino. "Reduction of Anxiety in Pediatric Patients: Effects of a Psychopedagogical Intervention Programme." *Patient Education and Counseling*, vol. 24, pp. 17–22, 1995.

Loening-Baucke, V. "Chronic Constipation in Children." *Gastroenterology*, vol. 105, no. 5, pp. 1557–1564, 1993.

Loening-Baucke, V. "Management of Chronic Constipation in Infants and Toddlers." *American Family Physician*, vol. 49, no. 2, pp. 397–413, 1994.

Lowsley, Oswald S., et al. *The Sexual Glands of the Male*. New York: Oxford University Press, 1942, p. 746.

Lyon, Richards P., and Sumner Marshall. "Urinary Tract Infection and Difficult Urination in Girls: Long-Term Follow-Up." *Journal of Urology*, vol. 105, pp. 314–317, February 1971.

Lyon, Richards P., and Donald R. Smith. "Distal Urethral Stenosis." *Journal of Urology*, vol. 89, pp. 414–421, March 1963.

Lyon, Richards P., and Emil A. Tanagho. "Distal Urethral Stenosis in Little Girls." *Journal of Urology*, vol. 93, pp. 379–388, March 1965.

Mahony, David T. "Studies of Enuresis—I: Incidence of Obstructive Lesions and Pathophysiology of Enuresis." *Journal of Urology*, vol. 106, no. 6, pp. 951–958, December 1971.

Mahony, David T., and Roland O. Laferte. "Studies of Enuresis—VII: Results of Distal Internal Urethrotomy in Girls with Juvenile Urinary Incontinence." *Urology*, vol. 4, no. 2, pp. 162–172, August 1974.

Mahony, David T., et al. "Incontinence of Urine Due to Instability of Micturition Reflexes: Part I—Detrusor Reflex Instability." Urology, vol. 3, pp. 229–239, 1980.

Mandell, Marshall. "Genitourinary Hypersensitivity in an Allergy Practice." (abstract). *28th Annual Congress of American College of Allergists*, Dallas, March 1972.

Mattelaer, J. J., and F. M. J. Debruyne. "Distal Urethral Stenosis in Young Girls." *Urologia Internationalis*, vol. 29, no. 5, pp. 389–398, 1974.

Matthiessen, T. B., et al. "A Dose Titration, and an Open 6-Week Efficacy and Safety Study of Desmopressin Tablets in the Management of Nocturnal Enuresis." *Journal of Urology*, vol. 151, pp. 460–463, February 1994.

McAninch, L. M. "External Meatotomy in the Female." *Canadian Journal of Surgery*, vol. 8, pp. 382–388, 1965.

McCarty, Eugene P., and Oscar L. Frick. "Food Sensitivity: Keys to Diagnosis." *Journal of Pediatrics*, vol. 102, no. 5, pp. 645–652, May 1983.

McDonald, H. P., et al. "Enuresis." *Fulton County Medical Society Bulletin*, September 3, 1953.

McDonald, H. P. "Enuresis." In H. F. Conn, ed., *Current Therapy*. Philadelphia: W. B. Saunders Co., 1961.

McDonald, H. P., et al. "Vesical Neck Obstruction in Children." *The American Surgeon*, vol. 27, p. 603, 1961.

McFadden, G. D. F. "Anatomical Abnormalities Found in the Urinary Tract of Enuretics, Their Significance and Surgical Treatment." *Proceedings of the Royal Society of Medicine*, vol. 48, p. 1121, 1955.

McGraw, Terry. "Preparing Children for the Operating Room: Psychological Issues." *Canadian Journal of Anesthesiology*, vol. 41, no. 11, pp. 1094–1103, 1994.

McGuire, E. J., and J. A. Savastano. "Urodynamic Studies in Enuresis and the Nonneurogenic Neurogenic Bladder." *Journal of Urology*, vol. 132, no. 2, pp. 299–302, August 1984.

McKendry, J. B. J., et al. "Enuresis—A Study of Untreated Patients." *Applied Therapeutics*, vol. 10, no. 12, pp. 815–817, December 1968.

McKendry, J. B. J., et al. "Primary Enuresis: Relative Success of Three Methods of Treatment." *Canadian Medical Association Journal*, vol. 113, pp. 953–955, November 22, 1975.

McLain, Larry G. *Current Problems in Pediatrics: Childhood Enuresis.* Chicago: Year Book Medical Publishers, 1979.

McNichol, Jane. *Your Child's Allergies: Detecting and Treating Hyperactivity, Congestion, Irritability, and Other Symptoms Caused by Common Food Allergies.* New York: John Wiley & Sons, 1992.

Meeks, John E. "Dispelling Fears of the Hospitalized Child." *Hospital Medicine*, pp. 77–81, October 1970.

Miguel, L. C., et al. "Enuresis and Urinary Pathology." *Cirrugia Pediatrica*, vol. 3, no. 3, pp. 112–116, July 1990.

Mikkelsen, Edwin J. "Chapter 42: Elimination Disorders." In Harold I. Kaplan and Benjamin J. Sadock, eds., *Comprehensive Textbook of Psychiatry*, 6th ed., vol. 2. Baltimore: Williams & Wilkins, 1995.

Mikkelsen, Edwin J. "Modern Approaches to Enuresis and Encopresis." In Melvin Lewis, ed., *Child and Adolescent Psychiatry: A Comprehensive Textbook*. Baltimore: Williams & Wilkins, 1991, chap. 50.

Miller, A. "Cysto-urethroscopy of Enuretic Children." *Proceedings of the Royal Society of Medicine*, vol. 49, p. 895, 1956.

Miller, Harry C. "Bedwetting Is Seldom Psychological." *Consultant*, p. 84, September 1972.

Miller, K., and G. T. Klauber. "Desmopressin Acetate in Children with Severe Primary Nocturnal Enuresis." *Clinical Therapeutics*, vol. 12, no. 4, pp. 357–366, July–August 1990.

Miller, Kenneth. "Concomitant Nonpharmacologic Therapy in the Treatment of Primary Nocturnal Enuresis." *Clinical Pediatrics*, Special Edition, pp. 32–37, 1993.

Moilanen, Irma, et al. "Personality and Family Characteristics of Enuretic Children." *Psychiatria Fennica*, vol. 18, pp. 53–61, 1987.

Morgan, Elaine. *The Descent of Woman*. New York: Stein & Day, 1972.

Morgan, G. Edward, Jr., and Maged S. Mikhail. "Chapter 44: Pediatric Anesthesia." *Clinical Anesthesiology*. Stamford, Conn.: Appleton & Lange, 1996.

Mori, Yoshinori, et al. "Congenital Lower Urinary Tract Obstruction and Enuresis in Children." *Nippon Hinyokika Gakkai Zasshi* (Japanese Journal of Urology), vol. 82, no. 3, pp. 481–487, March 1991.

Mori, Yoshinori, et al. "Treatment of Congenital Urethral Stenosis (Urethral Ring) in Children: Optic Internal Urethrotomy in Congenital Bulbar Urethral Stenosis in Boys." *Nippon Hinyokika Gakkai Zasshi* (Japanese Journal of Urology), vol. 80, no. 5, pp. 704–710, May 1989.

Mormon, J. A. G. "Congenital Bulbar Urethral Constrictions: Pathogenesis and Treatment of Diseases of the Bladder Neck and Urogenital Border Regions." *Urologia Internationalis*, vol. 30, no. 2, pp. 120–124, 1975.

Motoyama, Etsuro K., et al., eds. *Smith's Anesthesia for Infants and Children*, 5th ed. St. Louis: C. V. Mosby Company, 1990.

Mundy, Anthony R. "The Unstable Bladder." *Urologic Clinics of North America*, vol. 12, no. 2, pp. 317–328, May 1985.

Murphy, Selbritt, and Warren Chapman. "Adolescent Enuresis: A Urologic Study." *Pediatrics*, vol. 45, no. 3, pp. 426–431, March 1970.

Noguchi, C. T., et al. "Sickle-Cell Disease Pathophysiology." *Baillieres Clinical Haematology*, vol. 6, no. 1, pp. 57–91, March 1993.

Nørgaard, Jens P. "Urodynamics in Enuresis—I: Reservoir Function." *Neurourology and Urodynamics*, vol. 8, pp. 199–211, 1989.

Nørgaard, Jens P., and Jens C. Djurhuus. "The Pathophysiology of Enuresis in Children and Young Adults." *Clinical Pediatrics*, Special Edition, pp. 5–9, 1993.

Nørgaard, Jens P., et al. "Diurnal Anti-Diuretic-Hormone Levels in Enuretics." *Journal of Urology*, vol. 134, pp. 1029–1031, 1985.

Nørgaard, Jens P., et al. "Nocturnal Enuresis: An Approach to Treatment Based on Pathenogenesis." *The Journal of Pediatrics*, vol. 114, no. 4, Part II, p. 705, April 1989.

Nørgaard, Jens P., et al. "Nocturnal Studies in Enuretics: A Polygraphic Study of Sleep-EEG and Bladder Activity." *Scandinavian Journal of Urology and Nephrology* (supplementum), vol. 125, pp. 73–78, 1989.

Ornitz, E., et al. "Prestimulation-Induced Startle Modulation in Attention-Deficit Hyperactivity Disorder and Nocturnal Enuresis." *Psychophysiology*, vol. 29, pp. 437–451, 1992.

O'Regan, Sean, and Salam Yazbeck. "Constipation as a Cause of Enuresis, Urinary Tract Infection, and Vesico-Ureteral Reflux." *Medical Hypotheses*, vol. 17, pp. 409–413, 1985.

O'Regan, Sean, et al. "Constipation, Bladder Instability, Urinary Tract Infection Syndrome." *Clinical Nephrology*, vol. 23, no. 3, pp. 152–154, 1985.

Orwell, George. "Such, such were the Toys . . ." In *The Orwell Reader*, pp. 419–456. New York: Harcourt, Brace, 1953.

Oswald, Ian. *Sleeping and Waking*. Amsterdam: Elsevier Publishing Co., 1962.

Page, Harriet. "Jell-O Shows 'Life' When Subjected to EEG's in an Unusual Teaching Experiment." *Medical Tribune*, p. 9, March 3, 1976.

Palmtag, Hans, et al. "Functional Abnormality of 'Nonprovocative' Bladder Instability in Children." *Urologia Internationalis*, vol. 34, no. 3, pp. 176–183, 1979.

Parkkulainen, K. V. "Enuresis and Incontinence in Children." *Annales Chirurgie*, vol. 71, p. 221, 1982.

Pastinszky, I. "The Allergic Diseases of the Male Genitourinary Tract with Special Reference to Allergic Urethritis and Cystitis." *Urologia Internationalis*, vol. 9, pp. 288–305, 1959.

Penders, L., et al. "Enuresis and Urethral Instability." *European Urology*, vol. 10, pp. 317–322, 1984.

Perlmutter, A. D., et al. "Urethral Meatal Stenosis in Female Children Simulating Bladder-Neck Obstruction." *Journal of Pediatrics*, vol. 69, p. 739, 1966.

Petty, William Clayton. "Evolution of Safety in Anesthesia." *CRNA: The Clinical Forum for Nurse Anesthetists*, vol. 6, no. 2, pp. 59–63, May 1995.

Pfaundler, Meinhard. "Demonstration eines Apparatus zur seltatigen Signalisierung stattgehabter Bettnasung." *Verhandlungen der Gesellschaft fur Kinderheilkunde*, vol. 21, p. 219, 1904.

Pieretti, Raphael V. "The Mild End of the Spectrum of Posterior Urethral Valves." *Journal of Pediatric Surgery*, vol. 28, no. 5, pp. 701–776, 1993.

Pillay, Anthony L., et al. "Secondary Enuresis in Institutionalized Conduct-Disordered Children." *Psychological Reports*, vol. 64, no. 2, pp. 624–626, April 1989.

Pompeius, R. "Cystometry in Paediatric Enuresis." *Scandinavian Journal of Urology and Nephrology*, vol. 5, p. 222, 1971.

Powell, Norborne B. "Allergies of the Genito-Urinary Tract." *Annals of Allergy*, vol. 19, pp. 1019–1025, 1961.

Powell, Norborne B., et al. "Allergy of the Lower Urinary Tract." *Annals of Allergy*, vol. 28, pp. 252–255, June 1970.

Puri, V. N. "Urinary Levels of Antidiuretic Hormone in Nocturnal Enuresis." *Indian Pediatrics*, vol. 17, pp. 675–676, August 1980.

Rapp, Doris. *Is This Your Child? Discovering and Treating Unrecognized Allergies.* New York: William Morrow & Company, 1991.

Rapp, Doris. *Is This Your Child's World?* New York: William Morrow & Company, 1995.

Readett, D. R. "Determinants of Nocturnal Enuresis in Homozygous Sickle-Cell Disease." *Archives of Disease in Childhood*, vol. 65, no. 6, pp. 615–618, June 1990.

Richardson, Francis H. and Oliver G. Stonington. "Urethrolysis and External Urethroplasty in the Female." *Surgical Clinics of North America*, vol. 49, no. 6, pp. 1201–1208, December 1969.

Robson, William L. M., and Alexander K. C. Leung. "Side Effects and Complications of Treatment with Desmopressin for Enuresis." *Journal of the National Medical Association*, vol. 86, no. 10, pp. 775–778, 1994.

Roffwarg, Howard P., et al. "Preliminary Observations of the Sleep-Dream Pattern in Neonates, Infants, Children, and Adults." *American Journal of Psychiatry*, vol. 126, pp. 60–72, 1969.

Royal College of Physicians Committee on Clinical Immunology and Allergy. "Allergy: Conventional and Alternative Concepts." *Clinical and Experimental Allergy*, vol. 22, supplement 3, 1992 (entire issue).

Rubin, Lewis, and Murray B. Pincus. "Eosinophilic Cystitis: The Relationship of Allergy in the Urinary Tract to Eosinophilic Cystitis and the Pathophysiology of Eosinophilia." *Journal of Urology*, vol. 112, pp. 457–460, October 1974.

Rushton, H. Gil. "Evaluation of the Enuretic Child." *Clinical Pediatrics*, Special Edition, 1993, pp. 14–18.

Rushton, H. Gil., et al. "Predictors of Response to Desmopressin in Children and Adolescents with Monosymptomatic Nocturnal Enuresis." *Proceedings of the Second International Enuresis Research Center (IERC) Workshop: Pathophysiology and Treatment*, Aarhus, Denmark, May 27–29, 1995.

Ryan, C. F., et al. "Nasal Continuous Positive Airway Pressure (CPAP) Therapy for Obstructive Sleep Apnea in Hallermann-Streiff Syndrome." *Clinical Pediatrics*, vol. 29, no. 2, pp. 122–124, February 1990.

Sakurai, T., et al. "Lower Urinary Tract Obstruction and Subclinical Neurogenic Bladder in Childhood—III: The Urethral Ring Stenosis." *Nippon Hinyokika Gakkai Zasshi* (Japanese Journal of Urology), vol. 69, no. 6, pp. 743–753, June 1978.

Salzman, Louis K. "Allergy Testing, Psychological Assessment, and Dietary Treatment of the Hyperactive Child Syndrome." *Medical Journal of Australia*, vol. 2, pp. 248–251, August 14, 1976.

Saxton, H. M., et al. "Spinning Top Urethra: Not a Normal Variant." *Radiology*, vol. 168, no. 1, pp. 147–150, July 1988.

Scholtmeijer, R. J. "Chapter 7: Urethral Abnormalities in Enuresis and Urinary Infection." In J. H. Johnson and C. J. Scholtmeijer, eds., *Problems in Paediatric Urology*. Amsterdam: Excerpta Medica, 1972.

Schrott, K. M. "Enuresis: A Mainly Organic and Curable Disease in Childhood." *Zeitschrift Für Kinderchirurgie und Grenzgebiete*, vol. 19, p. 299, 1976.

Schultz, Nathan D., et al. *The Best Guide to Allergy*, 3rd ed. Totowa, N.J.: Humana Press, 1994.

Selig, Andrew Lee. "Treating Nocturnal Enuresis in One Session of Family Therapy: A Case Study." *Journal of Clinical Child Psychology*, vol. 11, no. 3, pp. 234–237, 1982.

Seth, R., and M. B. Heyman. "Management of Constipation and Encopresis in Infants and Children." *Gastroenterology Clinics of North America*, vol. 23, no. 4, pp. 621–636, 1994.

Shaffer, David, et al. "Behavior and Bladder Disturbance of Enuretic Children: A Rational Classification of a Common Disorder." *Developmental Medicine and Child Neurology*, vol. 26, pp. 781–792, 1984.

Sharma, Anjana, et al. "Behavioural Problems of Hyperactive Children." *Indian Journal of Clinical Psychology*, vol. 21, no. 1, pp. 6–10, March 1994.

Shaw, Charles R. *The Psychiatric Disorders of Childhood*. New York: Appleton-Century-Crofts, 1966.

Sher, P. K. "Successful Treatment of Giggle Incontinence with Methylphenidate." *Pediatric Neurology*, vol. 10, no. 1, p. 81, February 1994.

Shimada, K., et al. "Lower Urinary Tract Obstruction and Subclinical Neurogenic Bladder in Childhood: Relation to the Pathogenesis of Enuresis." *Nippon Hinyokika Gakkai Zasshi* (Japanese Journal of Urology), vol. 68, p. 636, 1977.

Shortliffe, Linda. "Primary Nocturnal Enuresis: Introduction." *Clinical Pediatrics*, Special Edition, pp. 3–4, July 1993.

Simonds, John F., and Humberto Parraga. "The Parasomnias: Prevalence and Relationships to Each Other and to Positive Family Histories." *Hillside Journal of Clinical Psychiatry*, vol. 4, no. 1, pp. 25–38, 1982.

Smith, A. D., et al. "The Wet-Bed Syndrome." *South African Medical Journal*, vol. 47, no. 40, pp. 1916–1918, October 13, 1973.

Smith, Anthony. *The Mind*. New York: Viking Press, 1984.

Smith, Donald R. "Critique on the Concept of Vesical Neck Obstruction in Children" (review). *JAMA*, vol. 207, no. 9, pp. 1686–1692, March 3, 1969.

Speer, Frederic. "The Allergic Child." *American Family Physician*, vol. 11, no. 2, pp. 88–94, February 1975.

Spence, H. M. "Urologic Aspects of Enuresis." *Southern Medical Journal*, vol. 34, p. 830, 1941.

Squires, Vicki L. "Child-Focused Perioperative Education: Helping Children Understand and Cope with Surgery." *Seminars in Perioperative Nursing*, vol. 4, no. 2, pp. 80–87, April 1995.

Steffens, J., et al. "Vasopressin Deficiency in Primary Nocturnal Enuresis." *European Urology*, vol. 24, no. 3, pp. 366–370, 1993.

Stein, Z. A., and M. W. Susser. "Nocturnal Enuresis as a Phenomenon of Institutions." *Developmental Medicine and Child Neurology*, vol. 8, pp. 677–685, 1966.

Stenberg, Arne, and Goran Lackgren. "Desmopressin Tablet Treatment in Nocturnal Enuresis." *Proceedings of the Second International Enuresis Research Center (IERC) Workshop: Pathophysiology and Treatment.* Aarhus, Denmark, May 27–29, 1995.

Stenberg, Arne, and Goran Lackgren. "Desmopressin Tablets in the Treatment of Severe Nocturnal Enuresis in Adolescents." *Pediatrics*, vol. 94, no. 6, pp. 841–846, December 1994.

Stenberg, Arne, and Goran Lackgren. "Treatment with Oral Desmopressin in Adolescents with Primary Nocturnal Enuresis: Efficacy and Long-term Effect." *Clinical Pediatrics*, Special Edition, pp. 25–27, 1993.

Stoffer, S. S. "Loss of Bladder Control in Hyperthyroidism." *Postgraduate Medicine*, vol. 84, no. 8, pp. 117–118, December 1988.

Susset, Jacques G., et al. "The Stop-Flow Technique: A Way to Measure Detrusor Strength." *Journal of Urology*, vol. 127, no. 3, pp. 489–494, March 1982.

Taub, S. J. "Enuresis Is Allergic in Origin in Many Instances." *Eye, Ear, Nose, and Throat Monthly*, vol. 48, no. 3, pp. 179–83, March 1969.

Taylor, John F. *Helping Your Hyperactive Child.* Rocklin, Calif.: Prima Publishing & Communications, 1990.

Thompson, Susan, and Joseph M. Rey. "Functional Enuresis: Is Desmopressin the Answer?" *Journal of the American Academy of Child and Adolescent Psychiatry*, vol. 34, no. 3, pp. 266–271, March 1995.

Tiret, L., et al. "Complications Related to Anaesthesia in Infants and Children: A Prospective Study of 40,240 Anaesthetics." *British Journal of Anesthesia*, vol. 61, pp. 263–269, 1988.

Unger, Donald L. "Urinary Tract Allergy." *Journal of Urology*, vol. 105, p. 867, June 1971.

Unger, Donald L., et al. "Urinary Tract Allergy." *Journal of the American Medical Association*, pp. 1308–1309, July 11, 1959.

Vanwaeyenbergh, J., et al. "Endoscopic Resection as Treatment of Enuresis with Posterior Urethral Valves." *Acta Urologica Belgica*, vol. 58, no. 1, pp. 133–137, 1990.

Von Hedenberg, C., and J. Gierup. "Urodynamic Studies of Boys with Disorders of the Lower Urinary Tract—II: Stenosis of the External Urethral Meatus: A Pre- and Post-Operative Study." *Scandinavian Journal of Urology and Nephrology*, vol. 11, no. 2, pp. 121–127, 1977.

Von Hedenberg, C., and J. Gierup. "Urodynamic Studies of Boys with Disorders of the Lower Urinary Tract—V: Posterior Urethral Folds: A Pre- and Post-Operative Study." *Scandinavian Journal of Urology and Nephrology*, vol. 15, no. 3, pp. 215–221, 1981.

Walsh, William. *The Food Allergy Book.* St. Paul, Minn.: ACA Publications, 1995.

Walter, C. K. "Allergy as a Cause of Genito-urinary Symptoms: Clinical Consideration." *Annals of Allergy*, vol. 16, pp. 158–159, 1958.

Warzak, W. J. "Psychosocial Implications of Nocturnal Enuresis." *Clinical Pediatrics*, Special Edition, pp. 38–40, July 1993.

Weider, Dudley J., et al. "Nocturnal Enuresis in Children with Upper Airway Obstruction." *Otolaryngology—Head and Neck Surgery*, vol. 105, no. 3, pp. 427–432, September 1991.

Whiteside, C. G., and E. P. Arnold. "Persistent Primary Enuresis: Urodynamic Assessment." *British Medical Journal*, vol. 1, no. 5954, pp. 364–367, February 15, 1975.

Wille, Søren. "Arftlighet Men Inte Psykisk Storning hos barn med nattenures." *Lakartidningen*, vol. 87, p. 2342, 1990.

Wille, Søren. "Comparison of Desmopressin and Enuresis Alarm for Nocturnal Enuresis." *Archives of Disease in Childhood*, vol. 61, pp. 30–33, 1986.

Wille, Søren. "Nocturnal Enuresis: Sleep Disturbance and Behavioral Patterns." *Acta Paediatrica*, vol. 83, no. 7, pp. 772–774, July 1994.

Wille, Søren, and I. Anveden. "Social and Behavioural Perspectives in Enuretics, Former Enuretics, and Non-enuretic Controls." *Acta Paediatrica*, vol. 84, no. 1, pp. 37–40, 1995.

Wille, Søren, et al. "Plasma and Urinary Levels of Vasopressin in Enuretic and Non-enuretic Children." *Scandinavian Journal of Urology and Nephrology*, vol. 28, no. 2, pp. 119–122, June 1994.

Williams, D. I., and R. C. Morgan. "Wide Bladder Neck Syndrome in Children: A Review." *Journal of the Royal Society of Medicine*, vol. 71, no. 7, pp. 520–522, July 1978.

Williams, Robert L., et al. "Chapter 23: Sleep Disorders." In Harold I. Kaplan and Benjamin J. Sadock, eds., *Comprehensive Textbook of Psychiatry*, 6th ed., vol. 2. Baltimore: Williams & Wilkins, 1995.

Winsbury-White, H.P. "Study of 310 Cases of Enuresis Treated by Urethral Dilatation." *British Journal of Urology*, vol. 13, pp. 149–162, September 1941.

Wyatt, J. K. "Distal Urethral Stenosis in the Female." *Canadian Family Physician*, pp. 47–50, December 1975.

Zaleski, Anne, et al. "Enuresis: Familial Incidence and Relationship to Allergic Disorders." *Canadian Medical Journal*, vol. 106, pp. 30–32, January 8, 1972.

Zapp, E. "Urologic Findings in Enuretic Children." *Deutsche Medizinische Wochenshrift*, vol. 89, pp. 372–379, February 21, 1964.

Zoubek, Jeri, et al. "Extraordinary Urinary Frequency." *Pediatrics*, vol. 85, pp. 1112–1114, 1990.

Zuckerberg, Aaron L. "Perioperative Approach to Children." *Pediatric Anesthesia*, vol. 41, no. 1, pp. 15–29, February 1994.

INDEX